CITYSPOTS
HELSINKI

**Barbara Radcliffe Rogers
and Stillman Rogers**

D1393530

Written by Barbara Radcliffe Rogers and Stillman Rogers
Original photography by Stillman Rogers
Front cover photography courtesy of Alamy Images

Produced by 183 Books
Design/layout/maps: Chris Lane and Lee Biggadike
Editorial/project management: Stephen York

Published by Thomas Cook Publishing
A division of Thomas Cook Tour Operations Limited
PO Box 227, Units 15/16, Coningsby Road
Peterborough PE3 8SB, United Kingdom
email: books@thomascook.com
www.thomascookpublishing.com
+44 (0)1733 416477

First edition © 2006 Thomas Cook Publishing
Text © 2006 Thomas Cook Publishing
Maps © 2006 Thomas Cook Publishing

ISBN-13: 978-1-84157-588-9
ISBN-10: 1-84157-588-7
Project Editor: Kelly Anne Pipes
Production/DTP: Steven Collins

Printed and bound in Spain by GraphyCems

CONTENTS

SYMBOLS & ABBREVIATIONS

The following symbols are used throughout this book:

🕿 telephone   📠 fax   ✉ email   🌐 website address
🄰 address   🕐 opening times   🄽 public transport connections

The following symbols are used on the maps:
🄸 Tourist Information Office
✈ Airport

Hotels and restaurants are graded by approximate price as follows:
€ budget price €€ mid-range price €€€ expensive

24-HOUR CLOCK

All times in this book are given in the 24-hour clock system used widely in Europe and in most international transport timetables.

⏵ *The Harbour and Market Square are the heart of Helsinki*

INTRODUCING
Helsinki

Introduction

Helsinki is a big dish of eye-candy. The greatest architects of their day (and ours) designed its buildings, which are set amid parks and against watery backdrops. And its beauty deserves a closer look, whether it's into the shop windows filled with smart Finnish design or inside buildings as stunning inside as out. But Helsinki is more – much more – than just another pretty face. It is a friendly, exciting, warm-hearted place filled with people whose wry wit will make you laugh and whose nightlife keeps you dancing into the night. It is blessed by almost round-the-clock sunlight in the summer, when no one seems to sleep, and a population that knows how to enjoy the long snowy winter. Join them on skis or snowshoes in the parks, on paths that glitter with lights reflecting in the snow, or skate across the frozen bay of Töölönlahti. Warming up is no problem – take a sauna (you can choose from traditional wood-fired or modern state-of-the-art spas), drink a steaming cup of *glogi*, go to a jazz club to hear authentic Dixieland, or dance to whatever moves your shoes.

The fastest growing capital in the European Union, Helsinki seems to be always on the move, with a star-studded line-up of festivals celebrating everything from samba and world cultures to heavy metal and Gay Pride. Downtown streets rock at night, and the buzz is of people having a good time, not trying to impress one another with their dress or their too-cool attitudes. Maybe that's because they know – and know the world knows it, too – that the Finns are at the head of the pack, whether its fashions or phones. Whatever, you'll see it here first, not because the Finns have rushed out to buy it, but because they have designed it themselves. That sense of living with fine design is so ingrained that Finns don't need to show off. But you'll sense that you are on the cutting edge, whether you're dining on the latest plates from Arabia, drinking out of the newest Iittala stemware, lounging in an Alvar Aalto chair or chatting on a Nokia.

It's hard not to have a good time in Helsinki, especially when things heat up at night. Perhaps that's the city's biggest surprise – and certainly what makes it so much fun to visit.

⬥ *Helsinki is a city full of cutting-edge design*

When to go

SEASONS & CLIMATE

With northern perversity, Helsinki's climate brings the most rain during the warm summer months, and the best chance of sparkling sunny days in winter. But neither season is extreme, with summer temperatures hovering around 68°F (20°C) and winter averages rarely dropping below 40°F (5°C). The most popular months to visit are between May and September, but the city is pleasant year-round, as long as you remember a raincoat in the summer and warm coat (and boots) in the winter.

Snow is frequent in winter, but rarely deep, often melting away quickly. Reflections on the snow make the city lighter during the short mid-winter days from November to January, when the sun doesn't rise until late morning and sets by 15.00.

ANNUAL EVENTS
January
DocPoint (late January–early February) Documentary festival featuring films from Finland, Baltic states and around the world. ❸ Fredrikinkatu 23. ❶ (09) 672 472. ❾ www.docpoint.info
International Ice Sculpture Competition (last two weekends of January) Competitors from around the world carve ice into artistic forms, on display until they melt. ❸ Helsinki Zoo, Korkeasaari. ❾ www.korkeasaari.fi ❽ Bus 11 or 16.

March
Musica Nova Helsinki Hear important new music from Finnish and international contemporary composers. ❸ Lasipalatsi, Mannerheimintie 22-2. ❶ (09) 6126 5100. ❾ www.musicanova.fi

Church Music Festival Kirkko Soikoon (mid-March) Churches honour Finnish and other Scandinavian sacred music in orchestral, choral and solo performances. ☎ (09) 709 2498.
Tickets: Ⓦ www.lippupiste.com or at the door.

April

April Jazz/Big Band Jazz Festival Finnish and international performers play in concerts halls, restaurants and other casual venues. ⊜ Ahertajantie 6 B, Espoo. ☎ (09) 455 0003.
Ⓦ www.apriljazz.fi

Vappu (30 April) This is Walpurgis Night, one of the biggest parties in Finland, when students wash the statue of Havis Amanda, the mermaid symbol of Helsinki, in champagne.

May

Vappu päivä (1 May) The Ullanlinna and Kaisaniemi quarters are the main sites for May Day celebrations with family-oriented fun, including carnivals.

● *Heavy snowfalls in the park don't deter Helsinki walkers*

Evening Markets Evening markets at the head of the harbour begin in mid-May, with local foods, handicrafts and other goods.

June

Helsinki Day (12 June) One of the few European capitals that knows its exact birthday, Helsinki celebrates with free concerts at Kaivopuisto Park, children's events, sports, tours and a market.
Ⓦ www.hel.fi/helsinkipaiva

Midsummer Eve Finns celebrate at country homes with huge bonfires and *jubanpusskalo* poles decorated with ribbons and flowers. Festival with bonfires, traditional folk music and dance; tickets at the Seurasaari bridge or in advance from Tomtebo Folklore Centre. Ⓐ Tamminiementie 1, Seursaari.
Ⓦ www.kolumbus.fi/seurasaarisaatio

July

Tuska Heavy Metal Festival Major bands from across Europe and the UK play in Kaisaniemi Park. Festival: Ⓦ www.tuska-festival.fi Tickets: Ⓦ www.lippupiste.com

Jazz Espa Free daily jazz performances on the Esplanadi, 16.00–18.00.

August

Helsinki City Marathon (mid-August) Scandinavia's biggest marathon begins at the Paavo Nurmi statue and winds along the shore and hillsides. Ⓐ Radiokatu 20. Ⓣ (09) 3481 2405.
Ⓦ www.helsinkicitymarathon.com

Koneisto Electronic Music Festival More than 100 artists have gathered for this event since 2001. Ⓐ Cable Factory, Tallberginkatu. Tickets: Lippupalvel. Ⓣ 0600 1 08 00. Ⓦ www.koneisto.fi

Helsinki Festival (late August–early September) Featuring prominent international artists in various venues and a festival tent. The Night of the Arts brings street music and art. ☎ 0600 900 900. ⓦ www.helsinkifestival.fi

Art Goes Kapakka (mid-August) Ten days of music and entertainment, totalling 250 performances and events in clubs, bars, restaurants, theatres and streets. ⓦ www.artgoeskapakka.fi

September
Helsinki International Film Festival Finland's largest film festival draws upwards of 14,000 to see films from all over the world. ⓐ Mannerheimintie 22-24. ☎ (09) 6843 5232. ⓦ www.hiff.fi

October
Herring Market (early October) Fishermen gather in Market Square to sell traditional herring products, a chance to sample local foods.
Sailing Ship Days (mid-October) Sailing vessels gather in the harbour.

November
Tampere Jazz Happening A chance to see some of the finest musicians from around the world in small club and concerts venues. ⓐ Tullikamarinaukio 2, Tampere. ☎ (03) 3146 6751. ⓦ www.tampere.fi
Winter Circus (November–early January) Hurjaruuth Dance Company at Boiler Hall (Pannuhalli) brings dance and performing arts. Cable Factory, Tallberginkatu 1 A. ☎ (09) 565 7250. ⓦ www.hurjaruuth.fi

December
Women's Christmas Fair (2–6 December,) An astonishing variety of

fine crafts, all created by Finnish women, fill a market hall at the Wanha Satama. 🕐 10.00–19.00

Turku Christmas Market (3–18 Dec,) In the Old Great Square, with crafts and foods. 🕐 12.00–18.00

Independence Day (6 Dec) This date kicks off the holiday season, also an occasion for processions, visits to cemeteries and gathering in churches and public places for concerts that always include Sibelius's *Finlandia*.

St Thomas Christmas Market The finest crafts, foods and arts line the Esplanadi, in colourful tents.

PUBLIC HOLIDAYS
New Year's Day 1 Jan
Epiphany 6 Jan
Easter 14–17 Apr 2006, 6–9 Apr 2007
May Day 1 May
Ascension Day 25 May 2006, 17 May 2007
Whit Sunday 4 June 2006, 27 May 2007
Midsummer Eve & Midsummer Day 23 & 24 June 2006, 22 & 23 June 2007
All Saints 4 Nov 2006, 3 Nov 2007
Independence Day 6 Dec
Christmas 25–26 Dec
(Shops open in the morning on Midsummer Eve and Christmas Eve)

◐ *The St Thomas Christmas market is a fixture in the city's calendar*

The National Romantics

By the turn of the 20th century, because Finland had never been independent – Sweden owned it until losing it to the Russians in 1809 – Finns were seeking a national identity and a cultural heritage of their own. The search lead them to their rural heartland of Karelia, whose folk-tales had already been gathered into a national saga know as the *Kalevala*. In the Karelian forests and lakes artists found inspiration in nature and in the tales of the *Kalevala* itself. They translated these into designs that are evident today in everything from stonework details in buildings to lighting fixtures and door hinges. These purely local motifs and themes were further shaped by the influence of the exciting new ideas of the Arts and Crafts Movement, which flowed in from Europe's cultural centres.

Into this exciting intellectual and political climate emerged a group of brilliant young architects, several only in their mid-twenties. Three of them – Herman Gesellius, Armas Lindgren and Eliel Saarinen – would become partners in some of the city's most prominent buildings. These names appear over and over again as designers of Helsinki's most outstanding architecture from this period.

The timing was perfect. Arts and Crafts/art nouveau styles and ideals neatly fitted Finland's goals of national identity and nationhood. These were styles that welcomed the native design motifs they drew from the Karelian forests, while at the same time representing all that was new and cutting-edge in modern Europe. The most evidence we see today is in the outstanding art nouveau (known in Finland by its German name, Jugendstil) architecture. But the National Romantic movement included painting, pottery, industrial design, fabrics, literature and even music (think of

Sibelius's *Finlandia*). At the Paris World Exposition of 1900, Finland – still a Grand Duchy of the Russian empire – surprised and impressed the world with its dramatic pavilion and the dynamic Finnish style that decorated it. These works of these 'National Romantics' are the beginning of what the whole world would come to admire as Finnish design.

⬤ *The elegance of 19th-century Finnish architecture is best seen on Esplanadi*

History

At a latitude of 60° north, Helsinki is the northernmost of all continental European capitals, with a prime location on the Baltic. Its position as the bridge between Russia and the west made Finland a pawn between the rulers of Sweden – Scandinavia's strongest and most aggressive power – and Russia. During Swedish rule the provincial capital was at Turku, and Swedish King Gustav Vasa, in order to compete commercially with Reval (now Tallinn) across the Baltic, established a trading port at Helsinki in 1550.

Originally farther up the Vanta River estuary, the community gradually moved downstream, so by 1640 it filled the peninsula where we find it today. Water surrounded three sides, so the busy port settlement gradually grew in importance, until the early 1700s dealt it a double blow: in 1710 the plague nearly wiped out its 2000 inhabitants and then in 1713 the Swedes burned it down to keep it from falling into the hands of Peter the Great's Russian troops. To protect the harbour from future attacks, Sweden built the great Suomenlinna fortress, but Russian harassment continued to slow the city's growth.

A century after the plague two more major events forever changed Helsinki. A fire in 1808 devastated most of the city and before it was rebuilt the province was ceded to Russia in 1809, forever ending Swedish rule. Finland became the semi-autonomous Russian Grand Duchy of Finland, and Tsar Alexander I lavished attention on his new city on the Baltic. He brought in the German-born architect C.L. Engel, who had designed many of the new buildings in St Petersburg. Engel redesigned Helsinki to give it its present elegant look. His influence is especially notable around Senate Square. In 1812 Alexander I moved the capital of the Grand

Duchy from Turku to Helsinki, and the city has been the capital ever since.

Rapid industrialisation from the 1860s to the beginning of the 20th century meant equally rapid population growth, and with it came the need for new neighbourhoods. Building after building sprang out of this boom, especially at the turn of the century, which gave Helsinki a remarkable number of art nouveau structures by Eliel Saarinen, Alvar Aalto and their contemporaries. At the same time, growing nationalism pushed the country toward independence.

Finland seized the moment when revolution rocked Russia in 1917. Parliament declared independence on 6 December and after a short period of civil unrest a republic was declared in 1919, with Helsinki as its capital. Since independence, with the exception of the period of Soviet invasion in the 1940s, Helsinki has prospered and grown as an industrial and design centre at the forefront of the Scandinavian design phenomenon. It has also been a centre for sports competitions since the 1952 Olympics, and a prime diplomatic venue for resolving international disputes. Since 1995 it has been a member of the European Union.

● *The ordeal of World War II is commemorated at Hietanemi Cemetery*

Lifestyle

Whatever other Scandinavians may imply, make no mistake that the Finns invented the sauna and are the undisputed experts on all things sauna-related. For most Finns, the chance to relax in a sauna is part of life's rituals, and they may enjoy one at any time of day – before breakfast, at bedtime, after skiing or going for a run, or whenever the spirit moves them. They conduct meetings in saunas, entertain family and friends in saunas and build them in their homes, in hotels, in cabins at the edge of lakes and even on little

● *There's nothing like a sauna by the lakeside*

houseboats. Having a lake handy is popular, since the Finns are great believers in a quick plunge into cold water after – or during – a sauna.

While the Finns have a reputation for not speaking much, they can be quite voluble in social situations, especially when loosened up with a little alcohol. They also have a wicked sense of humour, often very dry and sly – with a keen sense of the ridiculous. They can laugh at themselves, and their seeming self-depreciation is a popular national joke with them. It is true, however, that a group of Finns can sit in a room together without uttering a word, and be quite comfortable. So don't be alarmed if silence falls. And expect silence in the sauna, unless it's a business meeting. By the way, the latter will never be co-ed; saunas are always gender-divided except when shared by families. The same is true of the nude beaches in Helsinki, which you will find at Seurasaari and on Pihlajasaari. Women and men each have a separate section of beach for taking it all off.

Finns have a live-and-let-live attitude, so although Helsinki doesn't have the gay scene of Stockholm, gays are welcome and no one pays much attention. There are several gay clubs, but at most of them heterosexual couples are just as welcome. Their general attitude seems to be 'no big deal'. You'll find the Finns to be casual, but well dressed when they go out for an evening at nice places. They dress for the climate, so it's not unusual to see boots and thick ski jackets in the cloakrooms of upmarket restaurants in the winter. In fact, the Finns are pretty sensible people, who don't get huffy over dress codes (unlike Stockholm) or have bouncers stationed to keep out people who don't 'look the part' of a there-to-be-seen night scene. The Finns go out to have a good time, and they are happy for you to have a good time, too.

Culture

That Finland has such a distinct culture of its own is really remarkable, considering that this small country spent so much of its past being tossed back and forth between two other – and very strong – cultures. That the Finnish language has remained distinct and in steady use is equally surprising. Today, just enough of the Russian and Swedish flavours remain in Finnish culture to make things interesting, but never to predominate.

What does predominate is the Finnish sense of style. Leaders in modern design, the Finns are the epitome of the Scandinavian style – clean lines, fresh concepts, functional designs that look sharp and work well. Whether it's a building, a mobile phone, sportswear or a kitchen appliance, if it's designed in Finland, it will blend the often-conflicting needs of form and function into one graceful whole. Interest in design is more than a trade commodit, it's a national passion, because the Finns genuinely revel in being surrounded by well-designed things, whether they are the world's most comfortable scissors (Fiskars) or stylish home accessories (Marimekko or Arabia). Helsinki's design district is the place to revel in this Finnish phenomenon. There, in the space of a few streets, you'll find the DesignMuseo, the Museum of Finnish Architecture and the Design Forum, as well as galleries and designers' shops.

Other arts hold a high place in Finnish culture, too. Foreigners may be surprised to see enthusiastic fans of all ages in audiences at the opera or symphony. Finns are likely to have the works of Finnish artists hanging on their walls. Finland's architects are world famous,

● *The best of Finnish design, whether in fashion or ordinary household objects, is on show at DesignMuseo*

A RACE APART

Although Finland is certainly a Scandinavian country, and culturally has imbibed a lot from its long connection with Sweden, the Finns are not primarily of the same northern Germanic stock as their Scandinavian neighbours, and their language is also distinct. No one knows for sure how long the Finns have been living in the Baltic or exactly where their ancestors came from, but the Finnish language belongs to a group that includes Estonian and Hungarian, entirely unrelated to the Indo-European languages that nearly all of the rest of Europe speaks.

and the Finns value their creativity just as much as the rest of the world, so you'll see examples of their work at every turn. Helsinki residents are far more likely to know the name of a local building's architect than residents of any other city in Europe.

Helsinki is filled with performance venues for everything from opera and dance to rock concerts and sports competitions. Tickets are refreshingly well-priced – those for the Philharmonic Orchestra concerts are between €5 and €15, for example. For tickets to various concert and theatre venues contact Lippupalvelu (❶ 0600 1 08 00. Ⓦ www.lippupalvelu.fi), or Ticketti (❶ 0600 1 16 16. Ⓦ www.tiketti.fi). For schedules of everything from music and theatre to sports events, see *Helsinki This Week*. To learn about art galleries and shows, pick up an English copy of *Taide-Art*, a brochure complete with a map to help you find them.

▶ *Locals and visitors alike fill the city's streets and squares*

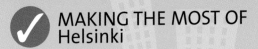

MAKING THE MOST OF
Helsinki

Shopping

WHERE TO SHOP

The streets bordering Esplanadi and the parallel Aleksanterinkatu
lead to Mannerheimintie, forming the centre of Helsinki's most
fashionable (and pricey) shopping district. Just beyond lies the design
district (don't miss the Design Forum for the hottest new looks in
everything from paper clips to coffee pots), and Fredrikinkatu, lined
with boutiques and music shops. In the morning market at the
harbour, you'll find fresh local farm products, crafts and Russian fur
hats, with more foods sold in the striped market hall. Another market
is at Hakaniemi, with crafts on the upper floor inside. At the western
edge of the city is the restored Hietalahti market hall and a giant flea
market where you can get anything from last year's clothing to
family heirlooms – all at cheap prices.

Shops are generally open Monday to Friday 09.00 or 10.00 to
18.00 or 20.00 and Saturday 09.00 to 14.00. Most close Sundays,
though major department stores often open Sundays June to August
and before Christmas.

WHAT TO BUY

Distinctive Finnish products to look for are glassware (big names are
Iittala, Nuutajarui and Arabia), clothing of fur and leather, traditional
and contemporary jumpers and jerseys, and beautiful wooden utensils
and furnishings. Exquisite kitchenware, carved in graceful and flowing
forms of velvet-smooth local woods include spoons, spatulas and cake
servers. Foods you may want to take back with you after you've tasted
them are preserves of cloudberries and lingonberries, smoked reindeer
or salmon, and the incomparable Finnish honey.

Local crafts, found in handwork and museum shops and in

markets, vary widely. Rustic reindeer made of bundled straw or hand-knit traditional woollen hats, socks and mittens are sold alongside the sleek, modern designs for which Scandinavia is so well known. In Helsinki's shops you'll find Sámi crafts from Lapland, such as reindeer-bone jewellery and carved birchwood cups. Look for the *duodji* label, assuring that these are genuine Sámi crafts.

VAT REFUNDS

Finland's 22 per cent VAT is often refundable for those who are not residents of the European Union. The easiest way to avoid receiving separate euro cheques from each shop (these may cost you more than their value to cash) is to use Global Refund Service. Ask for a refund cheque at any shop displaying a 'Tax Free' logo. At the airport, have these stamped at the Global Refund Desk and collect your refund in cash.

USEFUL SHOPPING PHRASES

What time do they open/close?
Milloin se avataan/suljetan?
Mil-loin she ervertahn/suljehtahn?

How much is it?
Paljonko se maksaa?
Perlyonko she merksah?

I'd like to buy ...
Haluaisin ostaa ...
Herlu-aisin ostah ...

Eating & drinking

It's true that Finnish cuisine has not yet hit the European charts, but several of Helsinki's chefs certainly have. The best of them revel in the ingredients of the surrounding water and land – seafood from the Baltic and from Finland's lakes, vegetables and berries whose flavours have concentrated as they ripen in the long hours of summer sun, wild berries from the north, mushrooms gathered from the forests, and game from the tundra and fells. A number of Helsinki's restaurants offer special seasonal menus of these local ingredients at the height of their season, as part of an initiative called HelsinkiMenu.

Complicated preparations are shunned for those that let the natural flavours of fresh ingredients shine through. Chefs draw on the traditional influences of Finland, Russia and Sweden, as well as an eclectic mix that ranges from Asian to Mediterranean. While you can find French, Italian, Chinese, Thai and even Irish pub food, you'll eat best when you seek Finnish chefs working with their own native ingredients.

LOCAL FARE

Meals are normally served in three courses, often beginning with a warming hearty soup in the winter. Pork, lamb and beef are common main course meats, and many menus offer reindeer in some form. Bear is usually served in Russian restaurants (Helsinki's are known for being better than those in St Petersburg), as a stew or smoked.

Baltic herring, *silakka*, is the favourite fish, fried, grilled, baked with layers of potato and cream or pickled as a snack. Herring is also smoked or marinated in a way similar to *gravadlax*, which is made

RESTAURANT CATEGORIES
Price ratings for restaurants in this book are based on the
average cost of a main course for one person.
€ Under €10 €€ €10–20 €€€ Over €20

with salmon. Arctic char, trout, salmon and whitefish are popular,
and crayfish are in season during August and September.

In the autumn, markets are piled high with woodland
mushrooms, most from Lapland, and chefs take full advantage of
this bounteous supply. Chanterelles are the tastiest of these, but
you'll see all sorts, in meat dishes or served on their own.

Sausages (*makkara*) are the snack food or choice, and you'll find
them sizzling on grills in markets and street stalls. They may be
made from pork or any other meat, and are always delicious.
Mustamakkara is a black sausage from Tampere, nearly always
served with sweet-tart lingonberry jam.

Lingonberries and the earthy-sweet cloudberries ripen in the
autumn, but you'll find them as jams and condiments, and in
desserts any time of year. Cloudberries are an especially rare
delicacy, but they will be on the menus of better restaurants,
frequently as a topping for puddings and ice cream. Pastries and
baked goods are excellent, and the Finns enjoy these with their
coffee at cafés and bakeries. Sweet coffee breads are popular, as is
karjalanpiirakat, a sweet pastry from eastern Finland, with a filling
of rice. Breads are varied and very good, ranging from dark rye to a
snowy-white bread made with potatoes. Crisp flatbreads are usually
made of rye flour.

Breads are always part of a full breakfast, a meal that is usually quite hearty, with a hot dish of eggs and meat and often porridge, or a buffet of cold cuts and cheeses – and plenty of coffee, although tea will always be available.

DRINKS

Wine is available at most restaurants, and some, such as Carelia and Sundmans, have outstanding wine lists. Local alcoholic drinks include vodka, schnapps and liqueurs made from local berries. Look especially for *lakka*, made of cloudberries, and *mesimarja*, which is made from highly-flavoured Arctic brambleberries. A good local beer is Lapin Kulta. In the winter you'll be offered *glogi*, a tasty blend of red wine, spices, raisins, almonds and blackcurrant juice. There are as many recipes for this as there are people making it, some using white wine. At any winter market, you'll find at least one steaming black cauldron of *glogi*.

MEAL TIMES

Breakfast is normally served from 07.00 to 10.00, and lunch begins early, at 11.00. The evening meal is also served early, often from 16.00 or 17.00, but continues late into the evening, with many restaurants

● *Finns make the most of the summer by eating outdoors as much as possible*

serving until 23.00. The midday meal may be a light lunch or a full meal. The latter is often a bargain, at a set price as low as €8. Advance booking is wise for popular restaurants, especially on Wednesday, Friday and Saturday evenings. If meeting Finnish friends for a meal (or any other occasion), remember that they are prompt and value punctuality. If you are delayed for more than five minutes, phone them – they will be carrying a mobile.

TIPPING

Service charges are usually included in restaurant bills, but a modest tip is always welcome if service has been attentive. Give this directly to the server in cash, rather than adding it to the bill.

USEFUL DINING PHRASES

I would like a table for ... people, please.
Saadaanko me pöytä ...?
Sahdahnko meh per-ewta ...?

May I see the menu, please?
Voinko mä nähdä menun?
Voin-ko mah nahkh-da mehnun?

May I have the bill, please?
Mä maksaisin laskun?
Mah merksaisin lerksun?

I am a vegetarian.
Olen kasvissyöjä.
Olehn kers-vis-sewer-ya.

Where is the toilet (restroom) please?
Missa on vessa?
Mis-sa on vehs-ser?

Entertainment & nightlife

With almost 10 per cent of its population university students, Helsinki is among Europe's hippest cities, with non-stop Gen-X nightlife that's all the better for being largely undiscovered by foreigners. Don't worry about feeling left out, though, since almost everyone under 40 speaks excellent English. Variety is the name of Helsinki's game, with clubs run by film directors, jazz clubs, gay clubs, raucous pubs and heavy metal karaoke bars.

CLUBS & BARS

Without the pretensions of Stockholm, but with all its variety and cool, Helsinki's night scene is user-friendly. No dress codes – you'll want to be smartly dressed, but no ties are required and no bouncers will be at the door selecting clientele on the basis of their designer labels. Age is another matter, since clubs set their own rules. If you're over 24, you're home free; between 20 and 24 you may not be allowed into some clubs, especially on busy nights. A few welcome anyone over 18, especially in the area around the Kaampi metro station, a popular area for under-20s.

The hot nights are Friday and Saturday, but Wednesday is also often busy. Expect to pay about €5 for admission to clubs, more for those with live music, plus another €1–2 for the compulsory coat check. A glass of beer or wine us usually about €4–5.

Nightlife is hottest in the streets around the centrally located railway station (forget the grungy areas that surround railway stations in may other cities – in Helsinki this is prime real estate), along the Esplanadi and immediately south, between Mannerheiminti and Fredrikinkatu, west of Mannerheiminti between Finlandia Hall and the opera, and in the streets south of

Uudenmaankatu, as far as Kapteeninkatu.

Do be aware that Finns can become belligerent when drunk, and fights may break out as night fades into morning. So if the atmosphere begins to take on an angry tone, slip quietly away, and under no circumstances engage a drunk in an argument or take chances with a potentially insulting remark. And if you are insulted, ignore it and leave as soon as possible.

PERFORMANCES

Clubs are not the only place young Finns spend a night out. Live performances are everywhere – arena rock shows, headliners, experimental metal, pop and a summer packed with festivals that always include music, often free.

Besides the highbrow halls for opera, ballet and classical music (all well attended by people of all ages), venues include the Savoy Theatre for stage performances by Finnish and touring companies that range from classical theatre to contemporary and occasional musical shows, Olympic Stadium (see page 89), home to all the big summer concerts, and the somewhat smaller Hartwall Areena, where even headliners like Metallica, Depeche Mode and Elton John perform. At the smaller House of Culture you'll hear metal, rock and pop.

Savoy Theatre ⊜ Kasarminkatu 46. ❶ (09) 169 3703.

Hartwall Areena ⊜ Areenakuja. ❶ (020) 41 997.

ⓦ www.hartwall-areena.com

House of Culture ⊜ Sturenkatu 4. ❶ (09) 774 0270.

CINEMAS

Cinema programmes are available from hotels and the tourist office. The widest choice is at Tennispalatsi, with 14 screens, and

Kinopalatsi, with 10. The selection is international and all films are shown in their original language with Finnish subtitles. Soundtracks are very rarely dubbed. The Orion is home to the Finnish Film Archive, showing three films every day except Mondays. Tickets at the major cinemas are about €10 for evening, smaller venues are less. Book ahead for Friday and Saturday evenings.

Tennispalatsi ⓐ Salomonkaru 15. ⓣ 0600 007 007.
Kinopalatsi ⓐ Kaisaniemenkatu 2. ⓣ 0600 944 44.
Orion ⓐ Eerikinkatu 15. ⓣ (09) 615 400. ⓦ www.sea.fi

TICKETS & INFORMATION

Helsinki City Tourist & Convention Bureau (see page 152) has up-to-date information on what's happening at all venues, including clubs. Before you go, visit ⓦ www.hel2.fi/tourism, and click on 'brochures' to download three publications filled with the latest news on what's hot in entertainment and clubs. *Groovy Nordic Oddity, Bohemian Nordic Oddity* and *Smooth Nordic Oddity* each contain 24 insider tips.

Pick up a copy of the monthly *City Lehti* for listings of current happenings – it's free at most shops and hotels. *Helsinki This Week* is also free, the tourist office's magazine in English, available everywhere. It is stronger in restaurant information and has a good calendar of events for the current month, in addition to timely seasonal features. For a complete listing of the many summer music festivals in Finland, see ⓦ www.festivals.fi

Tickets for events at most major venues are available through Lippupalvelu Ticket Service (ⓣ 0600 1 08 00. ⓦ www.lippupalvelu.fi)

● *Helsinki has a wealth of exciting live performance venues*

Sport & relaxation

Don't abandon your fitness routines in Helsinki – this is an exercise-friendly, do-it town, with parks and paths everywhere. The Finns are great walkers, runners, skiers, skaters and cyclists, so this is a good way to mingle with locals, too. The most popular running and walking routes are around Töölö Bay and the shore at Old Town Rapids. To enjoy the network of bike paths between sights, borrow a free Citybike (€2 deposit) from the green racks or rent bicycles (or skateboards) from Töölö Bay Recreational Centre.

In winter, you can also rent ski equipment and snowshoes at the Töölö centre and go on your own or take a guided hike (① 06 228 81500, ⓦ www.helsinkiexpert.fi). The Paloheinä Recreational Centre also offers rental skis, boots and poles. Trails, lit after dark, open as early as November and may have snow into April. Skating rinks are everywhere, but the Kallion Tekojäärata at Brahen Kenttä has music and rental skates.

Töölö Bay Recreational Centre ③ Mäntymäentie 1. ① (09) 4776 9760.
Paloheinä Recreational Centre ③ Pakilantie 124. ① (09) 4159 1177.

All that sparkling clean water surrounding the city will tempt anglers, and all they need is a traveller's fishing permit from Stockmann Department Store or a fishing shop. The shore around the Old Town Rapids is reserved for fishing (ⓦ www.ahven.net).

The best beaches are at Seurasaari, Suomenlinna and Pihlajasaari. The Olympic-size pools at the Swimming Stadium and the Mäkelänrinne Swimming Centre are open to the public, or you can combine swimming with a real cultural fix at Helsinki's oldest traditional swimming hall.

The recently restored Yrjönkatu Swimming Hall opened in 1928, and is used by people of all ages. Bathing suits are not worn, so men and women swim at different times; the schedule is available at most hotels.

You shouldn't miss the most Finnish of all activities – a sauna. Combine it with swimming at Yrjönkatu Swimming Hall, use your hotel's or enjoy the finest in tradition at the 70-year-old Kotiharju, Helsinki's last old-fashioned wood-burning (as opposed to electric) sauna: the cost is €7, plus €1.50 for a towel. To find more options, visit Ⓦ www.sauna.fi. Or for the ultimate luxury, steal away for a day or two of sauna and aromatic Aqua Therapy at Naantali Spa, a beautiful resort near Turku.

Yrjönkatu Swimming Hall ⓐ Yrjönkatu 21. ① (09) 310 87401.
Kotiharju ⓐ Harjutorinkatu 1. ① (09) 753 1535.
Naantali Spa ① (02) 445 5100. Ⓦ www.naantalispa.fi

◐ *All of Helsinki's large parks have ski trails*

Accommodation

For a Scandinavian capital, Helsinki offers some surprisingly moderate hotel rates. Of course you can luxuriate in grandeur, but there are more budget options here than in many other Nordic cities. Even the finest hotels, such as the Hotel Kamp, offer special promotions, which bring this crème-de-la-crème hotel into more budget-friendly range, especially on weekends. Always ask about these when booking.

Most hotels are centrally located, and nearly all are close to public transportation. Unlike the case in many cities, you needn't worry about staying close to the railway station, since this is an excellent neighbourhood in the midst of the best shopping and attractions.

Kaivokatu, a booking service located at the railway station, handles hotels, hostels and smaller guest houses. For information on hostels, contact the Finnish Youth Hostel Association.

Kaivokatu ❶ (09) 22881400. ❶ (09) 22881499.
Ⓦ www.helsinkiexpert.fi ❶ Open Mon–Fri 09.00–19.00, Sat 09.00–18.00, Sun 10.00–18.00 June–Aug; Mon–Fri 09.00–18.00, Sat 09.00–17.00 Sept–May.
Finnish Youth Hostel Association Ⓦ www.srm.fi

PRICE RATING
Price ratings for accommodation are based on the average rate for a double room for one night (usually including breakfast).
€ under €75 **€€** €75–150 **€€€** Over €150

HOTELS

Aurora € The hotel is a bit out of town but on the route to the airport. Facilities include a pool, sauna, gym and a restaurant and the rooms are spotless Scandinavian modern. They have especially good rates when you reserve by internet. ⓐ Helsinginkatu 50. ⓣ (09) 770 100. ⓕ (09) 770 10200. ⓦ www.hotelaurorahelsinki.com

Finn € Just over a half-kilometre (one-third of a mile) from the railway station, this is a small (27 rooms) but comfortable hotel and reasonably priced. All rooms have private facilities, TV and phone, some have private shower as well. A pool and saunas are next door. ⓐ Kalevankatu 3B. ⓣ (09) 684 4360. ⓕ (09) 684 43610. ⓦ www.hotellifinn.fi

Arthur €–€€ A handsome and recently refurbished small hotel within 300 m (330 yd) of the railway station and the best shopping; weekend rates for a standard double are under €100 and superior rooms only slightly more. It has a well thought-of restaurant on site. ⓐ Vuorikatu 19. ⓣ (09) 173 441. ⓕ (09) 626 880. ⓔ reception@hotelarthur.fi ⓦ www.hotelarthur.fi

Helka €–€€ Rooms here are attractive and comfortable. A business traveller's hotel, so rates are less expensive at weekends. All rooms have private bathrooms, TV and phones. The hotel has saunas and a whirlpool for relaxation and a bar and restaurant. Centrally located. ⓐ Pohjoinen Rautatiekatu 23. ⓣ (09) 613 580. ⓕ (09) 441 087. ⓦ www.helka.fi

Crowne Plaza Helsinki €€ The Crowne Plaza is a large, multi-storey, modern, glass-fronted building in the very centre of city life.

Beautifully appointed modern rooms have everything, including high-speed internet connections. Fitness facilities are impressive: a large pool, treadmills, stationary bikes, weight machines and nice locker rooms. **a** Mannerheimintie 50. **t** (09) 252 10000.
f (09) 252 13999. **w** www.crowneplaza-helsinki.fi

Cumulus Kaisaniemi €€ Another business travel hotel, close to downtown. Clean, comfortable and friendly. **a** Kaisaniemenkatu 7.
t (09) 172 881. **f** (09) 605 379. **w** www.cumulus.fi

Cumulus Olympia €€ A sister hotel to the Kaisaneimi, this one is a good place if you are interested in athletics. It is near the Olympic Stadium, and at the Urheilutalo Sports Centre next door bowling, swimming and ball games are available. It is also close to Linnanmäki Amusement Park and the Sealife Aquarium.
a Läntinen Brahenkatu 2. **t** (09) 691 51. **f** (09) 691 5219.
w www.cumulus.fi

Haaga €€ Large and modern, this hotel is about 5 km (3 miles) from the centre, about halfway between downtown and the airport but handy to Central Park, Korkeasaari Zoo, the National Opera and the Finnish National Museum. Full amenities are available. Tali golf course is only 2 km (1 mile) away. **a** Nuijamiestentie 10.
t (09) 580 7877 **f** (09) 580 78386. **w** www.bestwestern.com

Palace €€–€€€ This is a charming boutique hotel located right on the waterfront; many rooms have harbour views. It was built in the 1950s and retains much of the feel of Scandinavian modernism of

O *The Hotel Kämp is one of the city's best hotels*

that period. It is small (37 rooms) and intimate and only minutes by foot to the Market Square, ferries and downtown shopping.
🅐 Eteläranta 10. ☎ (09) 134 56656. 🖶 (09) 654 786.
🌐 www.palace.fi

Scandic Grand Marina €€–€€€ Elegant modern rooms in a brilliantly converted 1913 warehouse designed by architect Lars Sonck. Excellent location on the harbour, opposite the ferry terminal.
🅐 Katajanokanlaituri 7. ☎ (09) 16 661. 🖶 (09) 664 764.
🌐 www.scandic-hotels.com

Sokos Hotel Torni €€–€€€ Nicely located near the city centre, the 142-room Sokos is categorised as a four-star but has reasonable rates. Rooms have wireless internet and other facilities include four saunas, multiple restaurants and bars. It is only 300 m (330 yd) from the railway station and 500 m (550 yd) from the bus station.
🅐 Yrjönkatu 26. ☎ (020) 123 4604. 🖶 (09) 433 67100.
🌐 www.sokoshotels.fi

Kämp €€€ Stunningly restored, the 1887 grand hotel has service to match, in a superb location near the Esplanade. The breakfast buffet is outstanding. 🅐 Pohjoisesplanadi 29. ☎ (09) 576 111, (09) 5761 1999 (reservations). 🌐 www.luxurycollection.com/kamp

Rivoli Jardin €€€ Close to the Esplanade and to the activities of the central district, this elegant boutique hotel has 55 rooms with a wide range of business and personal comfort features. Apartments are available and you can even bring your dog.
🅐 Kasarmikatu 40. ☎ (09) 681 500. 🖶 (09) 656 988. 🌐 www.rivoli.fi

HOSTELS

Eurohostel € 255 beds in 135 rooms; singles, doubles, triples and family rooms are available. All new furniture and recently painted. Rooms have TV and there are self-catering facilities on each floor. Rates include a morning sauna. Shared bathrooms. ⓐ Linnankatu 9. ⓦ www.eurohostel.fi ⓝ Trams 2, 4.

Hostel Suomenlinna € If you are into fortresses, this may be the place for you. The island fortress was built by the Swedes and reinforced by the Russians as a primary defence for the city from invasion and is a fascinating sight in itself (see page 108). The hostel has 40 rooms, a café and self-catering kitchen. Showers and toilets are shared. It is only a 15-minute ferry ride from the city centre. ⓐ Suomenlinna C 9. ⓣ/ⓕ (09) 684 7471. ⓦ www.leirikoulut.com

Stadion Hostel € The hostel is a friendly and comfortable place, a part of the Olympic Stadium. it has 162 beds, available in dormitories and in private rooms. Breakfast is served in the caféteria from 06.30; guests have a kitchen available and a choice of nearby restaurants. ⓐ Pohjoinen Stadiontie 3 B. ⓣ (09) 477 8480. ⓕ (09) 477 84811. ⓦ www.stadionhostel.com ⓝ Trolley 3B from the railway station, 3T or 7A from Mannerheimintie, 3B or 3T from Silja Lines ferry and 4 from Viking Lines ferry. Ask the driver to let you off at Aurora Hospital, from where it's a 200 m (220 yd) walk.

CAMPSITE

Rastila Camping Camping in the city is possible here, a 15–20 minute ride from the railway station. ⓐ Karavaanikatu 4. ⓣ (09) 321 6551. ⓕ (09) 344 1578.

THE BEST OF HELSINKI

If you only have a few days to spend in Helsinki, you may be tempted to concentrate on the eastern half of the city centre, but you should try to make time to take in some of the sights of the western and northern areas and definitely take a harbour trip to see this fascinating metropolis from a different angle.

TOP 10 ATTRACTIONS
Here are ten sights and experiences you won't want to miss on any trip to the city.

- **Suomenlinna Fortress** A World Heritage Site out in the harbour (see page 109).

- **Boat trips around the Archipelago** Admiring the city from all angles (see page 106).

- **Uspensky Cathedral** The Russian presence (see page 69).

- **Kauppatori (Market Square) and Harbour** The real heart of Helsinki (see page 62).

- **Design Museum** Brilliant design, brilliantly shown (page 73).

- **Art nouveau buildings** The beginnings of the Finnish love affair with architecture (see page 68).

- **Seurasaari Open-air Museum** The way they were (see page 111).

- **Korkeasaari Zoo** Big cat heaven (see page 111).

- **Temppeliaukio** The church in a rock (see page 90).

- **Finnish design shops** The latest and coolest – see it here first (see page 20)

⬇ *The art nouveau style reached to even the humblest buildings*

Here's a quick guide to seeing the best of Helsinki, depending on the time available.

HALF-DAY: HELSINKI IN A HURRY

If you're unlucky enough to have only half a day, maybe free time on a business trip, you can still use it to absorb a lot of the sights and sounds of the city. Begin at the market, right at the head of the harbour, for a look at what you'll see on tonight's menu and a feel for the hearty, good-humoured Finns. Make a detour east to see the interior of Uspensky Cathedral before heading uphill from the market to Senate Square. On the way you can walk through the Street Museum to get a feel for the city's changing appearance. Head west on Aleksanterinkatu, past the smart shops, stepping into no. 44, the Pohjola Building, for a sampling of Finnish Jugendstil. Don't miss the big square bordered by the National Theatre, the Ateneum and Saarinen's landmark Railway Station. Beyond the station, take a left on Mannerheimintie, then left again to circle back to the harbour along the Esplanadi. This walk will take you to some landmark sights, the best of Helsinki's shops and some great cafés (Engel on Senate Square or Kapelli on the Esplanadi are local favourites).

1 DAY: TIME TO SEE A LITTLE MORE

If you have completed the morning's whistle-stop tour and have acquired a feel for the architecture, design and lively buzz of the city, use the afternoon to take a boat bound for the fortress island of Suomelinna. The 15-minute trip gives good city views – think of it as a mini-cruise – and once on the island you can explore the fortress buildings, watch the excellent film, visit the museums and craft studios, and walk the island paths for views of the city, surrounding islands, and the ships in the Gulf of Finland. In the evening, treat yourself to a dinner in one of Helsinki's restaurants specialising in local ingredients. Then hit the streets around Fredrikinkatu to learn what real nightlife is.

2–3 DAYS: SHORT CITY BREAK

You can add a lot more experiences if you have another day or two. The first stop should be the Design Museum, after which you will want to wander in the city's exciting 'Design District' to see what's at the cutting edge before it hits the shops all over Europe. Don't miss the Design Forum, where you can find top designers' work in all price ranges. Window-shop your way north on Fredrikinkatu or take a bus to Temppeliaukio, carved out of solid rock. Head back east toward the unmissable tower of the National Museum and Finlandia Hall, opposite it, before returning to the centre along busy Mannerheimintie. If you have another day, spend it visiting some of the excellent museums or head for the islands: either the open-air museum of Seurasaari or the Helsinki Zoo to see rare big cats, including snow leopards and Siberian tigers.

LONGER: ENJOYING HELSINKI TO THE FULL

A longer stay gives enough time to head out of the city for a day in old Porvoo or one of the many cruises among the islands. Or combine the two by cruising to Porvoo. After a few days walking the pavements, you'll be ready to relax in one of Helsinki's many parks, where you can snowshoe or ski in the winter and walk or cycle in the summer. After that, you'll be ready for the other Finnish obsession, a sauna. If your hotel doesn't offer one, choose one of the many public saunas and join the Finns as they relax.

Something for nothing

Not just free, but a great way to mingle with locals, enjoy music and be part of local life, planning your get-away for one of Helsinki's many festivals is a win-win. Since the majority take place during the most popular tourist season, book accommodation early.

The ultimate in syncretism is the confluence of Walpurgis Night (itself coinciding with pagan rites of spring), May Day, International Workers' Day and Finland's Student Day celebrating graduation. The

● *Students crowd into Senate Square – it's a festival, not a protest*

city welcomes spring (even if the day brings a late snowstorm) in a most un-Finnish way, by becoming one giant block party, with champagne, picnics and bands of liberated students wearing white hats. A cap is placed ceremoniously on the statue of Havis Amana the evening of 30 April, and champagne flows along with the goodwill, far into the night and all the next day.

The last weekend in May brings the World Village Festival (🌐 www.maailmakylassa.fi), two days of free stage performances, exhibitions, street musicians and sports in Kaisaniemi Park. Several stages feature performers from all over the world, many of them emerging artists that go on to fame. Past performances have included Sengalese hip-hop, Chilean reggae, Finnish folk rock and a Spanish ska/rock/flamenco/Rai group. Exotic food, folk crafts and exhibition booths demonstrate the power of civil action to make a fairer world, and an international buzz fills the city.

Helsinki-päivä, Helsinki Day, celebrates the city's birthday on 12 June, with free concerts, a three-day samba and dance festival with free performances and lessons, free cruises and tours and museums open free. It ends with a rock concert in Kaivopuisto Park, with a surprise pop-star guest. There are market stalls on the Esplanadi, free performances on the Espa stage all day and free admission to Suomenlinna fortress. Especially good for families with children, it is relatively alcohol-free and admission is free all day at Linnanmäki Amusement Park.

Each August a large stage is built below the sloping lawn of the observatory for the Kaivopuisto People's Festival, forming an amphitheatre for a free performance. It could be anyone from the Beach Boys to a symphony orchestra. The last Thursday in August is Night of the Arts, when museums and galleries stay open until late at night and the streets are alive with free musical performances.

When it rains

Helsinki is such an outdoor city, filled with leafy parks, broad avenues, street markets and pedestrianised shopping streets, that most travellers spend much of their time outside enjoying the long daylight hours. Three of its most famous sights – the islands of Suomenlinna, Seurasaari and the zoo – are open-air attractions. But a whole layer of the city is so hidden that even multi-time visitors might not know it exists under their feet. Beneath the centre streets, from the railway station to the Esplanadi, under Mannerheimintie to the Forum, and as far west as the bus station, lies a maze of connected underground passages lined with shops, cafés, restaurants, bakeries and food markets. Street musicians play, and escalators and stairs connect to the department stores, malls and services above.

The tunnels even offer direct access to transportation, connecting the train and bus stations and city transit lines. In cold or rainy weather you can literally spend a day shopping or browsing in the subterranean shops, the department stores of Stockmann and Sokos, the trendy shops of the Forum, and even the Academic Bookstore, without ever emerging.

The two department stores and the Forum shopping mall have their food stores on the subterranean level, better places to look for typical foods than in the tourist shops. Browse the shelves for wild berry preserves and the coolers for smoked fish and venison. Both departments stores have good sections for Finnish design, in both fashion and home furnishings, as well as sections for typical local products, including genuine Sámi-made goods.

The underground routes access at least two of Helsinki's architectural landmarks, the interior of Eliel Saarinen's Railway

Station and the Academic Bookstore, designed by Alvar Aalto. And close to their exits are two art museums well worth exploring on a rainy day: the Ateneum, with the country's best collections of Finnish and foreign art, and Kiasma, the Museum of Contemporary Art, featuring post-1960 Finnish works. (Without the visible landmarks of the world above, it is easy to lose your bearings in the tunnels, so signs help you find your way.)

The Academic Bookstore is a destination in its own right

On arrival

TIME DIFFERENCES

Helsinki follows Eastern European Time (EET). During Daylight
Saving Time (end Mar–end Oct) the clocks are put ahead 1 hour. In
the Finnish summer at 12.00 noon, time at home is as follows:
Australia Eastern Standard Time 19.00, Central Standard Time 18.30,
Western Standard Time 17.00.
New Zealand 21.00.
South Africa 11.00.
UK and Republic of Ireland 10.00.
USA and Canada Newfoundland Time 06.30, Atlantic Canada Time
06.00, Eastern Time 05.00, Central Time 04.00, Mountain Time
03.00, Pacific Time 02.00, Alaska 01.00.

ARRIVING

By air

Vantaa International Airport is 19 km (12 miles) north of the city
centre. The two-terminal (domestic and international) airport has
three shopping centres and numerous exchange bureaux and ATMs.
Finnair operates a shuttle (30 minutes) to Helsinki railway station
(€5.20) every 20–30 minutes, daily 05.00–24.00. Public buses (about
40 minutes) depart 06.00–01.00, every 10–30 minutes (€3.40).
Taxis deliver you and your luggage directly to your hotel for about
€30. An alternative gateway used by low-cost airlines such as
Ryanair is Tampere. Buses connecting with arrivals run to Helsinki
(railway station), one-way fare €25 and journey time 2½ hours.
Vantaa International Airport ❶ (02) 001 4636.
Ⓦ www.helsinki-vantaa.fi
Tampere-Pirkkala Airport ❶ (03) 383 5407. Ⓦ www.airpro.fi

By ship

The ferry and cruise ship docks are right in the centre of the city, within a few steps of the market, the Esplanadi, shopping streets and hotels.

By rail

Rail passengers arrive at one of Helsinki's great architectural landmarks, Eliel Saarinen's 1911 granite Central Railway Station. This busy terminus has a wealth of facilities – including restaurants and coffee-shops, ATMs, public card phones and its own shopping mall – and is right in the centre of the city. Unlike many other large European stations, it is located in a busy, safe and upmarket area.
ⓦ www.vr.fi/heo/eng/helsinki/helsinki_rtasema.htm

Driving

Traffic is light, roads are well marked (and free of tolls) and drivers polite. But unless you plan to travel outside the capital and into the countryside, a car is really not necessary because public transport is so good.

If you are from a left-hand drive country, be especially aware that in Finland, driving is on the right, and cars overtake on the left. Drivers bringing their own cars from the UK should be sure their lights are adapted to right-hand driving. Drivers from outside the EU should carry an International Driving Permit (available from local automobile clubs before leaving home), along with their national licence. Unless otherwise posted, the speed limit is 80 kph (50 mph) outside the city, 50 kph (30 mph) within city limits and 100–120 kph (60–75 mph) on motorways (the limit increases with the number of lanes). In the city, trams, bicycles and pedestrians have right of way over cars. Seatbelts are compulsory everywhere.

If you intend to travel by car in the winter, you should be familiar with handling a vehicle on snow-covered and icy roads and driving in winter storm conditions. Anywhere outside the city, be aware that reindeer and elk are formidable obstacles that can appear suddenly in the road at any time. Hundreds of people are killed in wildlife collisions annually, so slow down whenever you see one, and be especially careful at dusk or dark.

FINDING YOUR FEET

Few capital cities are as compact or as easy to get around in as Helsinki. The central sites surround the harbour, and the city is laid out in a tidy grid with broad avenues. Some of its most outstanding architecture is visible from the harbour, and its streets are lined with elegant old buildings. The city is clean, well lit and safe, with drivers who are careful of pedestrians.

The neat, sensible street plan makes finding addresses easy (and house numbers are marked on most local maps), although street names may defy pronunciation until you sound them out slowly. Pick up a free map at the tourist office, either at the airport or at Pohjoisesplanadi 19, near the harbour (see page 152). Here you can buy a Helsinki Card, economical if you plan to visit many sites or use public transport often (see Getting Around, page 57, for price comparisons). Be sure to also get a copy of the brochure *See Helsinki on Foot*, which has excellent neighbourhood maps.

ORIENTATION

The city wraps around the harbour, with Senatori (Senate Square) behind it, easy to identify by the round dome of the Cathedral. To the east the golden domes of Uspensky Cathedral, on a second hill, provide another easily spotted landmark, and to the west stretches the Esplanadi, a wide park bordered by elegant buildings. From the end of the Esplanadi, the broad Mannerheimintie heads north-west, alongside the railway station and the bay of Töölönlahti. Between that avenue and the bay are the unmistakable Finlandia Hall and Opera House, with the Parliament House and the tall tower of the National Museum as landmarks on Mannerheimintie's western side.

From this easily walkable nucleus, other neighbourhoods are

● *Trams will take you to the cathedral and nearly all the other city sights*

MEILAHTI

Nordenskiöldinkatu

Mannerheiminitie

Helsinginkatu

Stu

Linnankoskenkatu

← SEURASAARI

Sibelius Monument

Opera House

Sibelius Park

Runeberginkatu

Töölönlahti

El

Eläint

National Museum

Finlandia Hall

HIETANIEMI

Runeberginkatu

Parliament House

Cent
Railw
Stati

Mechelininkatu

Arkadiankatu

Mannerheiminit

Rautatiekatu

Frederikinkatu

Lönnrotinkatu

Bulev

Porkkalankatu

Ruoholahdenkatu

Uudenmaan

Helsinki Car Museum

nginkatu

KALLIO

Hameentie

Sörnäisten Rantatie

ahti

niemenkatu

Unioninkatu

KORKEASAARI

Pohjoisranta

Cathedral

Senatori

anterinkatu

Kauppatori

Uspensky Cathedral

Kanavakatu

KATAJANOKKA

Esplanadi

Harbour

Laivasillankatu

Kasarmikatu

N

0   500m

Tehta nkatu

UUNISAARI

SUOMENLINNA

easy to find: the art nouveau Katajanokka beyond Uspensky
Cathedral, Kallio north of Senate Square, Sibelius Park and
Hietaniemi to the west, Bulevardi to its south and the
neighbourhoods and parks of the southern end of the peninsula.
The three islands – Seurasaari, Suomenlinna and Korkeasaari – are
respectively west, south and east of the city. The handy website
Ⓦ www.kartta.hel.fi will locate any street address for you.

GETTING AROUND
Public transport

Buses, trams and trains make covering long distances easy, and the
website Ⓦ www.hel.fi has a Journey Planner section that gives you
exact bus and tram connections between any two points, including
scheduled times. *Helsinki This Week* has a transit map showing the

IF YOU GET LOST, TRY ...

Excuse me, do you speak English?
Anteeksi, puhutko englantia?
Erntehksi, puhutko ehnglerntier?

How do I get to ...?
Miten mä pääsen ...?
Mi-ten mah pa-a-sen ...?

Can you show me on my map?
Voitko näyttää minulle kartasta?
Voytko na-ewt-ta-a mul-leh ker-terster?

lines by colour. Buy tickets (€2) at stations or from the driver on the bus or tram; the ticket is good for transfers within an hour. If you expect to use public transit often, a tourist ticket for 24 hours is €5.40, for 3 days €10.80 and 5 days €16.20. Buy these at the railway station, ticket machines or from the tourist office.

Another option is the **Helsinki Card** (1 day €25, 2 days €35, 3 days €45), which also includes free admission to museums and attractions. But this is only a good value if you plan to visit several attractions, since admissions to most major sights are €5–8 each. Entrance to all the separate museums on Suomenlinna, plus the ferry trip adds up to more than a 24-hour Helsinki Card, but that assumes that you would tour every little museum in the complex.

Ferries shuttle continuously between the harbour and Suomenlinna (€5.50 return) and a little less frequently to Korkeasaari Zoo from the harbour or Hakaniemenranta.

Taxis

Hail taxis from the street (the yellow sign will be lit if it is available), or at busy times go to a taxi rank or phone ☎ (01) 000 700. The base rate is €4; most city destinations are €6–10. Tipping is not necessary, but if you do, add €1 to the fare.

Cycling

In good weather, consider cycling as a way to get between sights. The city is relatively flat and 900 km (over 500 miles) of cycle lanes and paths follow the major streets. Look for the free CityBikes in green racks, available for a € 2 deposit.

Outside Helsinki

Getting around Finland is easy and efficient using buses, trains or

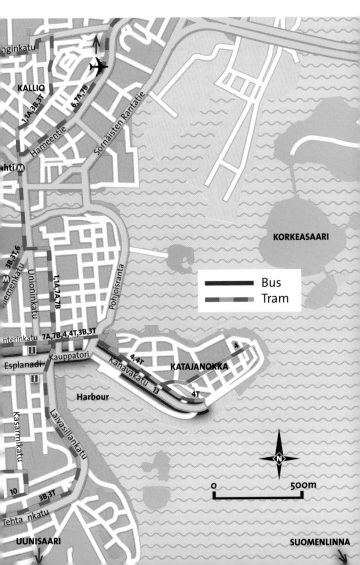

internal flights, but it can be expensive unless you fall into one of the discount groups. The fastest trains are the Pendolinos, connecting major points, such as Helsinki and Turku. Express trains connect to northern cities, such as Rovaniemi, an 11-hour ride. Eurail and other passes are valid in Finland (see page 143). Bus services are scheduled to be compatible with trains, reaching out into the countryside and smaller towns. Finnair flies to Rovaniemi and other points in the north, a much faster way to get there.

Train information ☎ (030) 720 902.

Bus information ☎ (02) 004 000.

Finnair ☎ (02) 031 40160. ⓦ www.finnair.com

CAR HIRE

All major companies are represented in Helsinki, most with desks at Vantaa airport. Check car hire rates before making air reservations, since you can often save with an air-car package from the airline.

If you plan to visit Helsinki before travelling elsewhere, consider picking up the car as you leave, instead of on arrival, to save city driving and parking charges. The minimum age for car hire is 18, and you must present (and carry while driving) your own home driver's licence. Non-EU residents should also have an International Driving Permit, obtained from an automobile club (you needn't be a member) before leaving home. In addition, you will need to show a credit card, even if you are not charging the car to one. If you plan to take the car on the ferry to Estonia or Sweden, be sure you have the necessary documentation (you should ask for this when you book).

🔘 *Snow lends enchantment to scenes of the city*

Esplanadi & the Harbour

So many of Helsinki's most popular sights are in the streets surrounding the harbour that it would be easy to spend several days in the city without venturing any farther. Outstanding architecture, churches, museums, dining and shopping are all within a few steps of the busy waterfront, itself a scenic attraction for the variety of ships and boats that seem to be constantly moving in and out.

SIGHTS & ATTRACTIONS

Half the fun of visiting Helsinki is the variety of sights and experiences. High on that list is just ambling around the harbour and through its markets, enjoying the architecture and the constantly changing waterscape. Each time you approach the harbour, it looks different, as the huge Baltic ferries and cruise ships come and go, and little boats sail in and out.

Kauppatori (Market Square)

At the harbour's edge, with some of its merchants selling directly from boats, is the colourful market, a daily gathering of locals, visitors, farmers, fishermen, craftspersons and traders. Impromptu cafés, enclosed by plastic in the winter, serve everything from juicy sausages to salmon fillets grilled on cedar planks. At the Esplanadi side of the harbour is Gustaf Nystrom's 1889 market, worth visiting for the market stalls of honey, smoked fish, local cheese and other delicacies.

🔴 Helsinki Harbour. 🕐 Mon–Fri 08.00–19.00, Sat 08.00–16.00. Outdoor market Mon–Fri 06.30–14.00, Sat 06.30–15.00, Sun (summer only) 09.00–16.00.

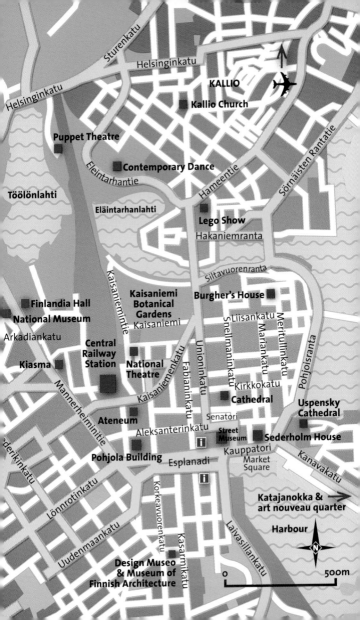

Sturenkatu

Helsinginkatu

Helsinginkatu

KALLIO

Kallio Church

Sörnäisten Rantatie

Puppet Theatre

Eläintarhantie

Contemporary Dance

Hämeentie

Töölönlahti

Eläintarhanlahti

Lego Show

Hakaniemranta

Siltavuorenranta

Kaisaniementie

Kaisaniemi Botanical Gardens

Kaisaniemi

Burgher's House

Liisankatu

Meritullinkatu

Snellmaninkatu

Mariankatu

Finlandia Hall

National Museum

Arkadiankatu

Central Railway Station

Kiasma

National Theatre

Kaisaniemenkatu

Fabianinkatu

Unioninkatu

Kirkkokatu

Cathedral

Pohjoisranta

Uspensky Cathedral

Mannerheiminitie

Ateneum

Aleksanterinkatu

Senatori

Street Museum

Sederholm House

derikinkatu

Pohjola Building

Esplanadi

Kauppatori
Market Square

Kanavakatu

Lönnrotinkatu

Korkeavuorenkatu

Katajanokka & art nouveau quarter

Uudenmaankatu

Harbour

Kasarmikatu

Laivasillankatu

N

Design Museo & Museum of Finnish Architecture

0   500m

Esplanadi

Stretching west from the Market Square, the open swath of the Esplanadi is bordered by elegant buildings. The pavilion at the beginning of the park is the Kappeli Restaurant, and the nearby bandstand is the scene of free summer concerts. Before Christmas, the entire Esplanadi is lined with booths selling crafts and food. Between it and Market Square, a statue of Helsinki's symbol, Havis Amanda, emerges from a fountain. The fountain is the work of Eliel Saarinen and Havis Amanda is by Ville Vallgren. On summer evenings, all of Helsinki seems to congregate and stroll in the park.

Senatori (Senate Square)

Up the hill behind the market, its dome visible above the row of intervening buildings, the majestic neo-classical Lutheran Cathedral is the focal point of Senate Square. The buildings at its adjoining sides, also by Engel, create an unusually unified public space – one of Europe's finest squares. It's a well used one, too, for celebrations that range from Finland's Independence Day to the start of the St Lucia Parade before Christmas. The early 19th-century cathedral, with its tall green dome, stands high above the square, at the top of a long flight of steps. Sederholm House, the oldest stone building in Helsinki, faces the lower corner of the square.

ⓐ Intersection of Unioninkatu and Aleksanterinkatu streets. Cathedral ⓒ Daily 09.00–24.00 summer; 09.00–18.00 winter. Admission free. ⓝ Bus/ tram 1, 3T, 3B or 4.

The Street Museum

You can walk all over the exhibits at one of the city's most unusual museums, which fills a street between Senate Square and Market Square. It's open 24 hours a day, and after dark the historic street

lighting shows the progression from early gas lamps to modern illumination. The streetscape moves from the early 1800s to the 1930s, with paving surfaces, lighting, street 'furniture' such as postboxes, lights and phone booths, many of them originals.
🅐 Sofiankatu. 🕐 Daily, 24 hours. 🅝 Bus/ tram 1, 3T, 3B or 4.

Helsinki Railway Station
For visitors arriving by rail or airport bus, the first stop is Helsinki's art nouveau railway station, designed by Eliel Saarinen. Its tower was the first of several designs that culminated in Saarinen's 1922 Chicago Tribune Tower, so it could be called the model for America's first skyscraper. Be sure to go inside to see the monumental arched halls, with walls ornamented in surprisingly delicate carved panels.
🅐 Rautatientori.

National Theatre
The focal point of the north side of the square beside the railway station is the National Theatre, built in 1902. The facade is in granite and sandstone, while the interior of the beautiful performance hall is almost entirely worked in curved lines. The foyer is decorated with fresco painting.

Kaisaniemi Botanical Gardens
The iron-framed glass Palm House was designed by Gustaf Nystrom in 1889, and more than 900 labelled plant species grow in rainforest, desert, Mediterranean and water environments. Go in the winter to be among orchids, African violets and water lilies with leaves two metres wide. The flowerbeds, fountains, pools and rose borders are beautiful in June, when the park hosts the Helsinki Pride festival.
🅐 Enter from Unioninkatu 44 or Kaisaniemenranta 2, near the

railway station. ☎ (09) 1911. Gardens ⏰ Mon–Fri 07.00–20.00, Sat & Sun 09.00–20.00 Apr–Sept; Mon–Fri 07.00–17.00, Sat & Sun 09.00–17.00 Oct–Mar. Glasshouses ⏰ Tues–Sun 10.00–17.00 Apr–Sept, Tues–Sun 10.00–15.00 Oct–Mar. Admission charge to glasshouses.

Pohjola Insurance Building

The interior motifs used in this 1901 office building by Saarinen, Lindgren & Gesellius are clearly Finnish, but the style shows the influence of French art nouveau. The dramatic sweeping staircase is asymmetrical, bordered in graceful balustrades. Art nouveau elements decorate these, as well as the walls and doorways of each landing, an example of the ideal of unity of a 'whole work of art'. To see the interior, go during weekday business hours, wait until someone opens the door and simply walk in.

ⓐ Alexsanterinkatu 44.

Privatbanken Jugendsali (Jugend Hall)

Jugendstil meets medieval in this 1904 interior by architect Lars Sonck. Romanesque churches seem to inspire the banking hall's low vaulting and three 'naves', but the similarities end there. Sonck uses the stone itself as a decorative material, sometimes rough-surfaced and rusticated, or polished to a high gloss in the muscular pillars. Relief carvings in their capitals are reminiscent of Viking ship prows, a popular Scandinavian theme but not frequently seen in Finland. Today the building houses the tourist office.

ⓐ Pohjoisesplanadi 19. ☎ (09) 169 2278. ⏰ Mon–Fri 09.00–17.00, Sun 11.00–17.00 Aug–June; Mon–Fri 09.00–16.00 July. Admission free.

⏵ *Katajanokka is an outdoor museum of art nouveau domestic architecture*

ART NOUVEAU

At the turn of the 20th century, a unique combination of
events, ideas and talents propelled Finland and its capital city
into the spotlight of European design. Finland's rising
intellectual and artistic community, already seeking their own
national identity (see page 14), was further inspired by the Arts
and Crafts Movement popular in Europe at the time. Today, the
results of that Golden Age of Finnish Art that resulted make
Helsinki a living museum of art nouveau, or Jugendstil as it
was known in German-speaking countries.

The primary architects were Lars Sonck, Sigurd Frosterus,
Selim Lindqvist, Valter Thome, Herman Gesellius, Armas
Lindgren and Eliel Saarinen. Helsinki was in a rapid growth
spurt, so housing and public buildings were in great demand –
and so were these brilliant young architects to design them.
Dozens of their landmark buildings cluster in easy-to-visit
neighbourhoods.

One of Europe's signature buildings in this style is
Saarinen's Helsinki Railway Station, whose dramatic straight
lines are accented by stylised figures holding lamps. The
interior is a triumph of art nouveau, combining elegantly
simple structure with flowing lines of natural ornamental
designs.

In the nearby downtown streets are several others; one of
the most outstanding is the Pohjola Insurance Building at
Alexsanterinkatu 44. You can't miss its rusticated stone
exterior, and its interior mixes stone with the local wood,
using designs of local plants and animals. Climb the curving

stairs to see art nouveau balustrades, doors, hinges, panels, even the newel post.

Just beyond the Uspensky Cathedral are some of the city's best residential examples. Katajanokka was the first neighbourhood of this type in Europe, and it is also Europe's best preserved. Walk along the streets of this five-block quarter, looking for details of stone ornament as well as surprising doorways, fanciful hinges, fairy-tale towers, balconies and other architectural details.

To see the best of Helsinki's art nouveau, sign up for the 'Pearls of Jugend' tour with Arch-Tours. Architect Marianna Heikinheimo or one of her associates will take you to the best art nouveau neighbourhoods and hard-to-reach out of town sites.
Arch-Tours ☎ (09) 454 3044. ✆ (09) 445 742.
🌐 www.archtours.fi

Uspensky Cathedral

Dominating the far side of the harbour is western Europe's largest Orthodox church, an ornate brick pile whose dome and towers are crowned by 13 gold cupolas. The interior is a wondrous cavern of icons, crosses, altars and gleaming gold, its intricately decorated arches offset by black marble columns. Along with serving the large Russian population, the church marks Helsinki's long-standing Russian influence. ➌ Kanavakatu 1. ☎ (09) 634 267. 🕐 Mon–Fri 09.30–16.00, Sat 09.30–14.00, Sun 12.00–15.00 May–Sept; Tues–Fri 09.30–16.00, Sat 09.30–14.00, Sun 12.00–15.00 Oct–Apr. Admission free. 🚌 Bus/tram 4, 4T, 13.

69

Katajanokka

The city's best concentration of art nouveau architecture is in the streets beyond Uspensky Cathedral, across the harbour from Market Square. Built within a decade at the height of Jugendstil's popularity, this is Europe's best preserved art nouveau residential neighbourhood. Each new apartment building, for the wealthy middle class who could afford quality design and construction, was designed to outdo its neighbours. The castle-like Aeolus building and the turreted Tallbergin Talo, across the street, form a gate to the quarter, at either side of Luotsikatu, which is lined with fine examples. Behind Tallbergin is another signature building, Eol, with a projecting balcony, corner turret and outstanding wooden door with elegant iron fittings and carved mythic creatures. The most exquisite doorway, however, is on the 1902 Kataja building, at Kaupiaankatu 2.

🚊 Bus/tram 4, 4T or 13.

Finlandia Hall

Famed architect Alvar Aalto's best known work in Helsinki is the enormous concert hall overlooking Töölö Bay. It's no accident that its white Carrara marble and black granite remind you of a piano keyboard. Tours of the 1970s building are given when the hall is not in use.

ⓐ Mannerheimintie 13e. ❶ (09) 402 41, Ⓦ www.fin.hel.fi ❶ Mon–Fri 09.00–16.00. Admission charge for tours. Ⓝ Bus/tram 4, 4T, 7 or 10.

Lego Show Helsinki

Adults have just as much fun at this Lego theme park as kids do. Admissions are ticketed in 3-hour time slots, 11.00–14.00, 14.00–17.00 and 17.00–20.00 with limited admissions for each, so the activities are never too crowded to enjoy, and there is plenty of

● *Finlandia hall is home to the Helsinki Philharmonic*

Lego – enough to go round for all the kids, large and small .
Coca Cola Centre, Sörnäisten rantatie 6 (Hakaniemi Market Square). (09) 2706 6640. Daily 10.00–20.00 May–Aug. Admission charge. Bus/tram 68, 23N or 97N.

Kallio Church

One of Finland's great architects, Lars Sonck, designed this great church in the National Romantic style in 1912. The bells inside its distinctive tower play a piece by Sibelius. Go inside the granite building to see the sculpted relief and other works of art, and go for a Sunday service or a concert to hear the great organs.
Itäinen Papinkatu 2. (09) 753 2086. Mon–Fri 12.00–18.00, Sat & Sun 10.00–18.00. Bus/tram 3B, 3T or 51.

CULTURE

A high concentration of the city's many museums lies in this central area; all are within easy walking distance of each other. The Helsinki Card admits visitors to nearly all of these, as well as to other attractions.

Ateneum

The building, which has recently been restored, is a beautiful setting for Finnish painting, sculpture, graphics and drawings, as well as international art. Internationally it is strong in works from the 19th and early 20th centuries, including those of Gauguin, Modigliani and Degas.
Kaivokatu 2 (opposite Railway Station). (09) 1733 6401.
Tues & Fri 09.00–18.00; Wed & Thur 09.00–20.00; Sat & Sun 11.00–17.00. Admission charge.

National Museum of Finland

Your first stop to learn about Finnish culture and traditions, the museum also covers Finland's history from prehistoric to the present. Historical artefacts and ethnographic collections illustrate daily life as well as events. Like the Ateneum, the building itself is a landmark, designed by the pre-eminent firm of Saarinen, Lindgren & Gesellius in 1902.

🅐 Mannerheimintie 34. 🕿 (09) 4050 9544. 🅦 www.fmnh.helsinki.fi 🕘 Tues & Wed 11.00–20.00; Thur–Sun 11.00–18.00. Admission charge. 🅝 Bus/tram 4, 4T, 7 or 10.

Museum of Contemporary Art (Kiasma)

The home of Finnish modern art is, like the city's other art museums, as much about the building as its contents. Designed by the American architect Steven Holl, the curvy Kiasma opened in 1998, and is considered one of Finland's paramount works of modern architecture – no small feat in the native land of so many well known architects. It contains a theatre for experimental drama, dance and music, as well as collections of post-1960 Finnish art.

🅐 Mannerheiminaukio 2. 🕿 (09) 173 36501. 🅦 www.fmnh.helsinki.fi 🕘 Tues 09.00–17.00; Wed–Sun 10.00–20.30. Admission charge; free Fri 17.00–20.30.

DesignMuseo

Nowhere is the evolution of decorative styles better illustrated than in the ground-floor gallery of this Design Museum. Decorative arts in ceramics, glass, metal, fabrics, furniture, utensils, and decor show how various style periods interpreted these items. So if you are unclear just how Victorian gave way to art nouveau and how that morphed into art deco and modernism, you can see side-by-side examples. Although the primary focus is on Finnish design, special exhibitions may feature other designers or themes. The shop is a treasure box of quality design gifts and books.

⊙ Korkeavuorenkatu 23. ❶ (09) 622 0540. ⓦ www.designmuseo.fi ⓛ Daily 11.00–20.00 June–Aug; Tues 11.00–20.00, Wed–Sun 11.00–18.00 Sept–May. Admission charge. Ⓝ Bus 17 or tram 10.

Museum of Finnish Architecture

Special exhibitions highlight Finnish architects past and present, as well as the styles they created and influenced.

⊙ Kasarmikatu 24. ❶ (09) 8567 5100, ⓦ www.mfa.fi ⓛ Tues, Thur–Sun 10.00–16.00, Wed 10.00–20.00. Admission charge. Ⓝ Bus 17 or tram 10.

Burgher's House

The oldest wooden building surviving in central Helsinki, the 1818 home is furnished and decorated to show how a middle-class family would have lived in the mid-1800s.

⊙ Kristianinkatu 12. ❶ (09) 135 1065. ⓛ Sun–Thur 11.00–16.00 June–Aug and Dec. Admission charge; free Thur. Ⓝ Bus/tram 1 or 18.

Sederholm House

Overlooking Senate Square, this is the central city's oldest stone building, from 1757. It contains exhibitions from the City Museum.

⊙ Aleksanterinkatu 16–18. ❶ (09) 169 3625. ⓛ Wed–Sun 11.00–17.00. Admission charge; free Thur. Ⓝ Bus/ tram 1, 3T, 3B or 4.

RETAIL THERAPY

The Esplanadi and the streets north – Mannerheimintie,

Aleksanterinkatu and Kaisaniemenkatu – are lined with the smartest shops, featuring the best in Finnish design. Just browsing their stunningly arranged windows is an art experience. On Senate Square and the streets around it you will find boutiques selling handicrafts and folk arts. In good weather, Market Square is filled with stalls of crafts and other local goods. You could shop till you drop without leaving this small area of Helsinki.

Stockmann Even an entire city block can't hold all the merchandise, which overflows into the Academic Bookstore, across Keskuskatu (and connected by a tunnel), in a building designed by Alvar Aalto. ⓐ Corner of Aleksanterinkatu and Mannerheimintie.

Sokos Slightly less rarified than Stockmann, but with a wide variety of high-quality Finnish and Scandinavian goods, from fashions to furnishings, Sokos is near the railway station. ⓐ Mannerheimintie 9.

Marimekko Famed for striking decorator fabrics, Marimekko also leads the design world with tableware, bags and wearables. ⓐ Pohjoisesplanadi 2 and 31, and other locations.

Aarikka Finland Clever, irresistible creations from wood include Christmas decorations, home decor, jewellery and whimsical utensils. ⓐ Pohjoisesplanadi 27.

Artek Furniture designed by Alvar Aalto forms the centrepiece, with other interior decor including rugs, linens, decorator fabrics and tableware. ⓐ Etelaesplanadi 18.

Design Forum To see – and buy – what's new and hot, shop at

Design Forum, where useful items from notebooks to kitchen appliances are practical, as well as beautiful and stylish, proving that Finnish design isn't just another pretty face. ❸ Erottajankatu 7. ❶ (09) 6220 8130. ❶ Mon–Fri 10.00–19.00, Sat 10.00–18.00, Sun 12.00–18.00.

Ril's Shop Brilliant fashion designer Ritva Liisa Pohjalainen believes that good design should 'work in all sizes' and that it begins with colour and fabric. So she starts by designing the fabrics, which are made in Italy, then creates very stylish, but wearable clothing. ❸ Pohjoisesplanadi 25. ❶ (09) 174 500.

CHRISTMAS MARKETS

Every Finnish school child knows that Santa lives in Finland, just south of Rovianemi, near the Arctic Circle. Many have visited him there. The village where he lives with his elves and reindeer, is open all year, except 24 December, but you don't have to go all the way to the Arctic Circle to find the Finns celebrating the Christmas season.

It begins early in December with the Christmas market that springs up like a little village on the Esplanadi. Helsinki's St Thomas Market forms a double row of bright tents, each outlined in tiny twinkling white lights. Step inside each one to find a tiny, brightly lit shop filled with beautiful handmade gifts: woodcarvings, knit hats and mittens, gingerbread, wrought ironwork, fanciful candles, woven scarves, wooden toys, fur hats, blown glass or jars of shimmering lingonberry jelly.

Brightly painted wooden puzzles come in shapes of fish, turtles, rabbits and hedgehogs. Velvet-smooth wooden cooking utensils – spatulas, forks, spoons and spreaders – are carved in graceful flowing shapes, from richly grained woods. Cups are formed from the gnarly-grained tree burls and cutting boards show off a variety of local woods in contrasting stripes. More rustic are the Christmas elves made of small angle-cut logs, with beards of curly yarn and peaked caps of bright felt. Smaller elves of wool perch everywhere.

A warmer venue for a craft show is the Women's Christmas Fair (🕒 Daily 10.00–19.00, 2–6 Dec), at the Wanha Satama, across Helsinki's harbour. The variety is astonishing, from stacks of beeswax candles and creamy Finnish honey to elegant painted silks, hobby-horses, finger puppets, fashionable knitwear and cheery little red-hatted elves, all created by Finnish women.

Kiseleff House Small shops sell Finnish handicrafts, from elegantly simple sauna accessories to toys and fashion. 🅐 Aleksanterinkatu 28.

Little Russia Brightly painted folk art (including nesting dolls) joins lacquer work, amber, antiques and icons, as well as Russian porcelain. 🅐 Aleksanterinkatu 24 (Senate Square). 🕒 Daily 09.00–20.00.

Hakaniemi Market Hall Textiles and handicrafts fill the small shops on the upper floor above the food hall. A daily open-air market lines the square outside. 🕒 Mon–Fri 08.00–18.00, Sat 08.00–16.00. 🚍 Bus/tram 68, 23N or 97N.

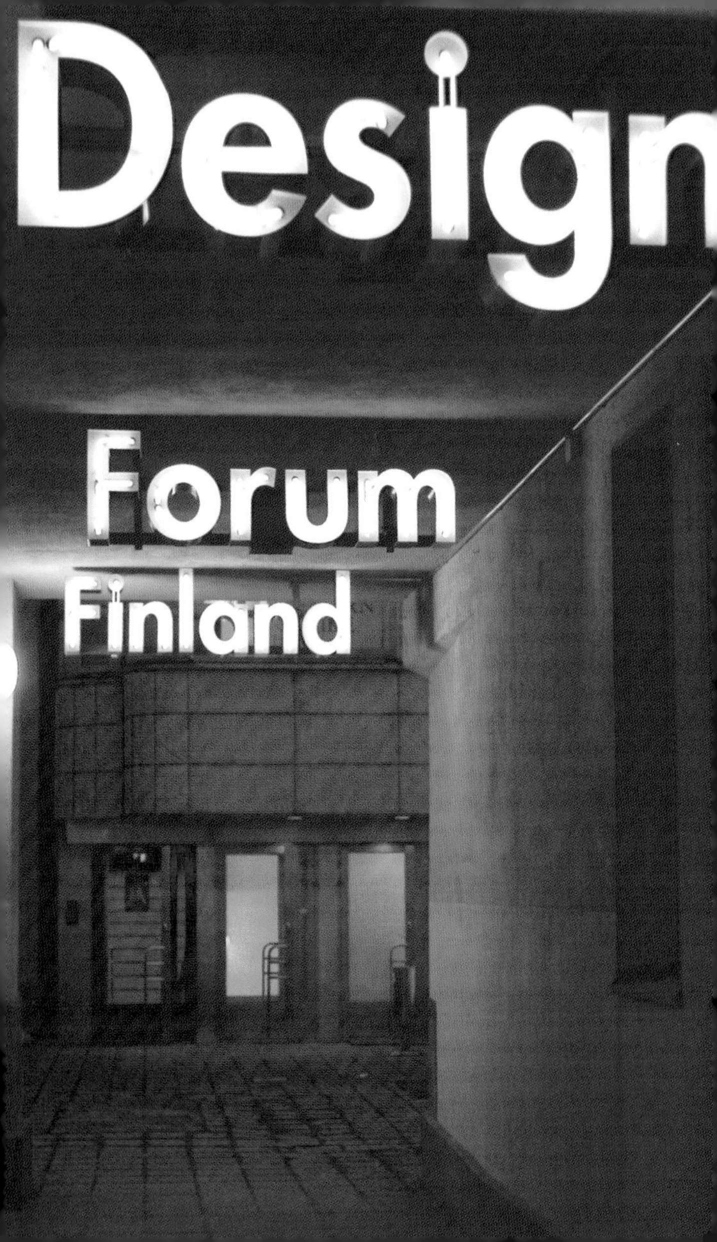
Design
Forum
Finland

TAKING A BREAK

Central Helsinki is filled with cafés, from elegant Old World settings to cafés in shops, museums and even a ship in the harbour. In the summer many of move outdoors to enjoy the long daylight hours.

Café Aalto On the balcony of the Academic Bookstore, the café overlooks the interior designed by Finnish design-meister Alvar Aalto. Relax with a book over coffee or have lunch here. The pastries are baked in-house. ⊜ Pohjoisesplanadi 39. ☎ (09) 121 41. ⏱ Mon–Fri 09.00–21.00, Sat 09.00–18.00.

Café Ateneum In the Museum of Finnish Art, the smoke-free café serves inexpensive vegetarian dishes at lunch, along with soups, sandwiches and pastries. ⊜ Rautatientori. ☎ (09) 1733 6231. ⏱ Tues & Fri 10.00–17.30, Wed & Thur 11.00–19.30, Sat & Sun 11.00–16.30.

Café Engel In the dark days of a northern winter, this cheering café is brightly illuminated with 'daylight' bulbs. The coffee menu is long and the lingonberry pie is mouthwatering. ⊜ Aleksanterinkatu 26. ☎ (09) 652 776. ⏱ Mon–Fri 07.30–24.00, Sat 09.30–24.00, Sun 11.00–24.00. ⊗ Bus/tram 1, 3T, 3B or 4.

Café Esplanad You'd expect high prices at this Esplanadi terrace, but the sandwiches, pastries, soups and salads are quite reasonable. Add smokeless air and occasional live jazz, and it's no wonder the place is popular. Minimum age is 20 in the evenings. ⊜ Pohjoisesplanadi 37. ☎ (09) 665 496. ⏱ Mon–Sat 08.00–22.00, Sun 10.00–22.00.

⊙ *The Design Forum is Finland's shop window to the world*

Exotic African dishes are served at lunch in this favourite hang-out of foreign students. ❸ Caisa cultural centre, Kaisaniemenkatu 6 B (near the Railway Station). ❶ (09) 692 5331. ❷ Mon–Fri 10.00–18.00.

Kappeli The beautiful building is a Helsinki landmark, and in the summer its terrace is always filled – especially during concerts on the adjacent Espa stage. Cakes are stunning (and stunningly pricey), and the cellar pub serves the café's own beer. ❸ Etelaesplanadi 1. ❶ (09) 681 2440.

Kathrina Few places are as warm and cosy on a winter day as the hold of this sailing ship. Wide benches invite curling your feet up to enjoy the hearty soups (the bread and milk are included), or a cup of hot chocolate. ❸ Market Square. ❶ (09) 320 9468. ❷ Daily 06.00–18.00.

Kauppatorin Kahvila In a bright orange tent in the market, but warm inside even on blustery snow-filled days, this is a favourite of local politicos, who come for the coffee and the outstanding meat pies. ❸ Kauppatori. ❶ (09) 411 10284. ❷ Mon–Sat 06.00–14.00.

Piccolo Piazza It may look like a neighbour's kitchen, but the pizza is good – and cheap, as are the pasta dishes. ❸ Merisotilaantori 3E (in Katajanokka). ❶ (09) 175 384. ❷ Mon–Fri 11.00–20.00, Sat & Sun 12.00–20.00. ❷ Tram 4 to the end of the line.

Renessance The minute you inhale the air, you know they bake their own pastries; sample the Finnish speciality, a sugar bun called *pulla*. Lunchtime soups are substantial and warming. ❸ Unioninkatu 18. ❶ (09) 666 366. ❷ Mon–Fri 09.00–23.00, Sat & Sun 12.00–23.00.

Restaurant Eliel You might not choose a railway station for a meal, but this café is very popular with locals and visitors for good food and low prices. Breakfast is served until late morning, the buffet lunch until late afternoon; there's a full menu evenings.
ⓐ Rautatieasema. ❶ (09) 707 4943. ❺ Mon–Sat 07.00–24.00, Sun 08.00–24.00.

⬥ *Café Kappeli – a landmark on the Esplanadi*

AFTER DARK

Friday and Saturday are the big nights for partying, but Wednesday is also popular for clubs. Book ahead for dinner at the more popular restaurants in the city centre at weekends or in the summer.

Restaurants

Saslik €€ Excellent Russian food, traditional decor and live Russian music celebrate Helsinki's ties with neighbouring Russia. Classic Russian dishes include *blinis*, bear and Strawberries Romanov. ⓐ Neitsytpolku 12. ⓣ (09) 742 55500. ⓝ Tram 10.

Fish Market €€–€€€ The sleek, light interior is inviting, as is the menu. Start with scallops with passionfruit marmalade and choose from fish mains such as roasted whitefish with goat's cheese cream and a dark sherry sauce. ⓐ Pohjoisesplanadi 17. ⓣ (09) 1345 6220. ⓛ Mon–Fri 11.30–15.00, 18.00–24.00, Sat 17.00–24.00.

Sasso €€€ From the smart, stylish doorway on Market Square to the stunning presentation, Sasso combines Italian cooking with Finnish design. It's a happy mixture, and the food is always paramount, as Nordic ingredients join imported Italian. ⓐ Pohjoisesplanadi 17. ⓣ (09) 1345 6240.

Sipuli €€€ The skylight looks straight up at the domes of Uspensky Cathedral. Nordic ingredients from the sea and forest are elegantly prepared – a frothy pumpkin soup is sprinkled with roasted nuts, and fried scallops are paired with fennel purée and pomegranate vinaigrette. ⓐ Kanavaranta 7. ⓣ (09) 622 9280. ⓛ Mon–Fri 18.00–24.00. ⓝ Bus/tram 4, 4T or 13.

G. W. Sundmans €€€ One of Finland's oldest restaurants, and still one of its best, Sundmans occupies a beautifully restored former mansion. Art nouveau interior details are soon forgotten as the food arrives, from the heavenly terrines with woodland mushrooms to the dessert of Arctic cloudberries. ⓐ Etelaranta 16 (facing the harbour). ⓣ (09) 622 6410. ⓛ Mon–Fri 11.00–14.30, 17.00–24.00, Sat 18.00–24.00.

Entertainment

Finlandia Hall Classical music fills the programme at Finlandia Hall, home venue of the Helsinki Philharmonic Orchestra (Helsingin kaupunginorkesteri) and the Radio Symphony Orchestra (Radion sinfoniaorkesteri). ⓐ Mannerheimintie 13e. ⓣ (09) 402 41. ⓦ www.fin.hel.fi ⓛ Mon–Fri 09.00–16.00. ⓝ Bus/tram 4, 4T, 7 or 10.

Helsingin Kaupunginteatterin Tanssiryhmä (Contemporary Dance Theatre) Finland's largest modern dance ensemble performs at various city stages, but mostly at the Helsinki City Theatre. ⓐ Eläintarhantie 5 in Hakaniemi, across Eläintarha to the north of the railway station. Tickets: ⓐ Ensi linja 2. ⓛ Mon–Fri 09.00–18.00. ⓐ Eläintarhantie 5. ⓛ Sat 12.00–19.00, day of performances. ⓣ (09) 394 022, ⓦ www.hkt.fi ⓝ Trams 1, 1A, 3T, 3B, 7A or 7B.

Kinopalatsi For American mainstream and occasional European films, check the 10 screens at this new multi-level cinema complex near the Railway Station. Tickets are discounted for weekday matinées. Cafés, wi-fi, shops and game arcades complete the centre. ⓐ Kaisaniemenkatu 2. ⓣ (09) 0600 94444. ⓦ www.kinopalatsi.fi ⓛ Daily from 11.00.

Nukketeatteri Vihreä Omena (Puppet Theatre) About 300 shows are performed each year, about 100 of them in the theatre's in-town home venue. Advance booking is a good idea, since many shows are sell-outs. 🅐 Eläintarhan Huvila 7. 🕿 (09) 712 818. 🕒 Mon–Fri 09.00–16.00.

Suomen Kansallisbaletit (National Ballet) Performances are at the Opera House, a state-of-the-art performance venue completed in 1993. Ballet favourites as well as lesser-known works are performed, with leading choreographers. 🅐 Helsinginkatu 58. 🕿 (09) 4030 2211. 🆆 www.operafin.fi 🕒 (Box office) Mon–Fri 09.00–18.00, Sat 15.00–18.00. Tram 3B, 3T, 4, 7A, 7B or 10.

Suomen Kansallisooppera (National Opera) The dozen productions each season include many classical favourites. The modern stage is among Europe's finest, with revolving floor, flexible mirrored ceiling and other techno tricks. Behind the scene tours are offered Tuesday and Thursday at 14.30. Tickets begin as low as €12, and some performances are free. 🅐 Helsinginkatu 58. 🕿 (09) 4030 2211. 🆆 www.operafin.fi 🕒 (Box office) Mon–Fri 09.00–18.00, Sat 15.00–18.00. 🚋 Trams 3B, 3T, 4, 7A, 7B or 10.

Bars & clubs

Arctic Icebar & UNIQ Inside the nightclub, Arctic Icebar is sponsored by Finland's own vodka, Finlandia. Try the ultimate chilled cocktail in a year-round environment of -5°C (23°F). They'll outfit you in warm clothes. There's a price for this big chill – €10 a drink plus the UNIQ cover charge at weekends. UNIQ itself offers disco and dancing. 🅐 Yliopistonkatu 5. 🕿 (09) 278 1855. 🆆 www.uniq.fi 🕒 Wed–Sat 22.00–04.00.

Bar and Library, Hotel Kamp The Hotel Kamp is the classiest place in town, and this is its classiest place for a drink. Forbes voted it among the best hotel bars in the world and you won't disagree. Kamp Brasserie and Wine Bar is a nice venue for a glass of wine, with 100 varieties sold by the glass from €4. ➌ Pohjoisesplanadi 29. ➊ (09) 576 1111.

Helsinki Club Large and stylish, the nightclub of the Hotel Helsinki has five bars and a dance floor. Occasional live music replaces the usual DJ playing Euro hits. Pay admission on busy nights; minimum age 24. ➌ Kluuvikatu 8. ➊ (09) 131 401. ➍ Sun–Tues 23.00–04.00, Wed–Sat 22.00–04.00.

Kaarle XII Off the tourist path, this huge complex contains bars, restaurants and plenty of Finnish pop. Go Thursday to Saturday, when it rocks, but the minimum age is 24. ➌ Kasarmikatu 40. ➊ (09) 612 9990. ➍ www.kaarle.com. ➍ Tues–Sat.

Kerma The place to meet hip locals in a relaxed setting with a small dance floor. Music is different nightly, from house to hip-hop. ➌ Erottajankatu 7. ➊ (09) 680 2665.

Osafat A very young set hangs out at this disco in the Kallio section, past the railway station. ➌ Cumulus Hotel, Läntinen Braahenkatu 2. ➊ (09) 69 151. ➍ Until 03.00. ➍ Bus/tram 3B, 3T or 51.

Ravintola Fennia Step through the over-the-top ornate doorway to discover restaurants, bars and clubs. On the Rocks is hard rock with live bands, Baarikarpanen caters to an older crowd. ➌ Mikonkatu 17 (near the Railway Station).

Western & northern Helsinki

The broad Mannerheimintie slices the part of Helsinki lying north of the Esplanadi neatly in half. Although it may seem as though everything you could want is on the harbour (eastern) side of that line, there is a lot more to see if you cross it. Fewer museums and attractions, perhaps, but more of the city's colourful nightlife and a great deal of its shopping lie in the streets adjoining Uudenmankatu, Lonnrotinkatu and the shopping street of Frederikinkatu. Some of the city's most frequently visited attractions are in this area. Among these are the Church in the Rock, the Olympic Tower and Finland's most popular amusement park.

SIGHTS & ATTRACTIONS

Sibelius Monument

The great Finnish composer once said that 'Nobody erects a monument to a critic' – and thus expressed a frustration of artists everywhere. He needn't have worried about his own legacy – not only a monument, but an entire Sibelius Park to accommodate it – although the critics had much to say about the monument. Designed by Eila Hiltunen, it was unveiled in 1967, and was immediately subjected to a barrage of criticism. Composed of a collection of large metal pipes that catch the wind, the monument creates its own music. Later, in response to the complaints that people didn't 'identify' with the composer through this monument, a more conventional statue of him was added. The park is a nice place to stroll or take a picnic.

ⓐ Sibelius Park, Mechelininkatu 38 (Taka-Töölö). ⓛ Daily, daylight hours. Admission free.

Linnanmäki &
Sea Life Centre

Vauhtitie

Winter
Gardens

MEILAHTI

Nordenskiöldinkatu

Mannerheimintie

Olympic
Stadium

Helsinginkatu

Eläintarhantie

Linnankoskenkatu

Sibelius
Monument

Opera House

Sibelius
Park

Runeberginkatu

Töölönlahti

Runeberginkatu

Hietaniemi
Cemetery

Mechelininkatu

Temppeliaukio

Kunsthalle
Helsinki

Mannerheimintie

Central
Railway
Station

N

Arkadiankatu

500m

Museum
of Cultures
& City Art
Museum &
Tennispalatsi

Mannerheimintie

Forum

Rautatiekatu

Frederikinkatu

Länsiväylä

Albertinkatu

Lönnrotinkatu

Bulevardi

Ruoholahdenkatu

Porkkalankatu

Uudenmaankatu

Iso Roobertinkatu

Sinebrychoff
Art Museum

Cable Factory

Tehtaankatu

Helsinki Car
Museum

⬤ *Some like it, some don't, but you can't ignore the Sibelius Monument*

Hietaniemi Cemetery

On All Saints, Christmas and Independence Day, Finns visit
cemeteries not only to remember loved ones, but also to honour
national heroes and those fallen in wars. Along with the public
observations, it's a personal thing with many Finns to remember
those who died for their country or who contributed to culture or

public life. Hietaniemi is especially busy on 6 December, Independence Day, when the march of students to Senate Square begins here. Buried in its elegant park setting, along with a clutch of presidents in Statesman's Grove, is Marshal Mannerheim, Commander-in-chief of Finnish forces in the war that gained Finland freedom from Russia in 1939. Architects Alvar Aalto and Engel and artist Albert Edelfelt rest on Artists Hill.

ⓐ Mechelininkatu. Ⓝ Tram/bus 8, 15A.

Temppeliaukio (Church in the Rock)

Nowhere is the Finns' fascination with architectural experiments more evident than in the Church in the Rock, one of the city's most visited attractions. The notion of carving an entire church out of solid rock is not new, but such troglodyte chapels are rarely cut into a relatively small outcrop in the middle of a city. However, that's exactly what architects Timo and Tuomo Suomalainen did, covering the excavation with a roof of woven copper connected to concrete spokes. The rounded copper roof offsets the deadening effect of the granite walls, creating extraordinary acoustics for concerts, which can range from Christmas chorales to klezmer groups.

🅐 Lutherinkatu 3. 🕿 (09) 494 698. 🕒 Mon, Wed 10.00–17.00, Tues 10.00–12.45 and 14.15–17.00, Thur & Fri 10.00–20.00, Sat

---

🔻 *The city's most unusual church was hollowed out from living rock*

10.00–18.00, Sun 11.45–13.45 and 15.30–18.00. Hours may vary to accommodate services and concerts. Admission free.

Olympic Stadion (Stadium)
Built in 1938 by functionalist architects Yrjö Lindegren and Toivo Jäntti, for the 1940 Olympics, the stadium was not used because World War II intervened and the Games were cancelled. It was not until the summer of 1952 that the Olympics finally came to the stadium, which is now a venue for athletic and music events. Outside is a statue of runner Parvo Nurmi, 'The Flying Finn', who won the gold medal, and carried the Olympic torch the last lap into the stadium for the 1952 Olympiad. The stadium's 72 m (236 ft) tower gives a panoramic view of the city and over the Gulf of Finland, and also at the stadium is the Museum of Finnish Sports.
ⓐ Paavo Nurmentie 1. ☎ (09) 436 601. ⓦ www.stadion.fi Museum of

Finnish Sports ❶ (09) 434 2250. ⓦ www.urheilumuseo.org
🕐 Tower: Mon–Fri 09.00–20.00, Sat & Sun 09.00–18.00 (closed during events). Admission charge. Museum: Mon–Fri 11.00–19.00, Sat & Sun 12.00–16.00. Admission charge. ◍ Tram/bus 3T, 3B, 4, 4T, 7A or 7B.

Kaupungin Talvipuutarha (Winter Garden)

Near the Olympic Stadium, this vast collection of glasshouses is a tropical paradise perfect for a winter's day. Step inside to stroll beneath towering palms and Norfolk Island pines, and to revel in the passion flowers and camellias that bloom through the winter. Christmas and Easter bring indoor displays of flowers and in the summer the outdoor rose gardens are spectacular.
ⓐ Hammarskjöldintie 1. ❶ (09) 166 5410. 🕐 Tues 09.00–15.00, Wed–Fri 12.00–15.00, Sat & Sun 12.00–16.00. Admission free.
◍ Tram 8.

Linnanmäki Amusement Park

From the original 1951 wooden roller coaster to the latest in high-tech thrills, Linnanmäki is fun for all ages. In addition to the 17 major rides and 14 kiddie rides, the park has a fun house, hall of mirrors and a toy museum. The park is run by group of children's charities and ticket money goes to a good cause. Live shows are performed daily on the outdoor stage and a free play area, Fairytale Valley, is always there for children.
ⓐ Tivolikuja 1. ❶ (09) 773 991, ⓦ www.linnanmaki.fi. 🕐 May–early Sept, hours vary. Admission free, rides charged separately or with general pass.

▶ *The Olympic Tower is the epitome of 30s style*

Sea Life Helsinki

The underwater world of the local Baltic waters, the Arctic and the tropical seas are explored in this series of underwater exhibits. A transparent tunnel takes visitor through these undersea worlds to see creatures from starfish to sharks. Environmental impact of human activity is a major theme, dealing with issues such as pollution and unrestrained harvest of fish. Be there for the feeding times at 12.30 for tropical reef (Wednesday 18.00) and 14.30 for the ocean tank.
ⓐ Tivolitie 10. ⓣ (09) 565 8200. ⓦ www.sealifehelsinki.fi
ⓛ Thur–Tues 10.00–17.00, Wed 10.00–20.00 Oct–Apr; Mon–Sat 10.00–19.00, Sun 10.00–17.00 May–June and Aug–Sept; daily 10.00–20.00 July. Admission charge.

CULTURE

Three art museums and one highlighting Finland's relation to other world cultures are located in the streets west of Mannerheimintie, an area more known for its shopping and nightlife than its traditional attractions.

At the far western edge, the Cable Factory is a multi-faceted complex of small museums, with a theatre and restaurant.

Museum of Cultures

The 'Fetched from Afar' exhibit, new in 2005, is a permanent feature of this museum of ethnic cultures, and it makes the museum more interesting to visitors, since it explores the Finno-Ugric peoples (see page 22), as well as telling the story of other cultures through the work of early Finnish explorers and anthropologists. Part of the exhibit is the early China collection, brought to Finland by traders and seafarers in the early 19th century.

🅐 Tennispalatsi, Salomonkatu 15 (near the bus station).
🅣 (09) 405 09806. 🕒 Tues–Thur 11.00–20.00, Fri–Sun 11.00–18.00.
Admission charge; free Tues 17.00–20.00.

Helsinki City Art Museum

Special exhibitions of Finnish and international art are shown here,
often part of an international circuit.
🅐 Tennispalatsi, Salomonkatu 15 (near the bus station).
🅣 (09) 310 87001. 🆆 www.taidemuseo.hel.fi 🕒 Tues–Sun
11.00–20.30. Admission charge.

Kunsthalle Helsinki

Changing exhibitions of contemporary art highlight young artists as
well as those who have already established a reputation. Taidehallin
Klubi, the gallery's restaurant, is open for lunch and evening meals
Monday–Saturday and through the evening. The bar is open
Monday–Saturday until 02.00.
🅐 Nervanderinkatu 3. 🅣 (09) 454 2060. 🆆 www.taidehalli.fi
🕒 Tues–Fri 11.00–18.00, Sat & Sun 12.00–17.00 mid-June–Sept.
Admission charge.

Sinebrychoff Art Museum

Finland's finest collection of Old Masters and other European art
from the 1300s to the 1800s is displayed in the furnished mansion
of the museum's donors. The rooms, although used as galleries, have
fine parquet floors and other interior features. Miniatures and
porcelain collections are especially impressive.
🅐 Bulevardi 40. 🅣 (09) 1733 6460. 🆆 www.sinebrychoffintaidemuseo.fi
🕒 Tues & Fri 10.00–18.00, Wed & Thur 10.00–20.00, Sat & Sun
11.00–17.00. Admission charge, free Thur 17.00–20.00. 🆃 Tram 6.

Helsinki Car Museum

If model cars race your engines, don't miss Europe's largest collection of over 3000 miniature autos. The real things are there, too, and the collection of vintage autos – everything from a 1931 taxi to the cars of Finnish presidents – is enlivened by wax figures of the famous Finns who owned them. ⓐ Munkkisaarenkatu 12. ⓣ (09) 667 123. ⓛ Tues–Sun 12.00–15.00 Apr–Oct; Thur–Sun 12.00–15.00 Nov. Admission charge. ⓝ Tram 6.

Kaapelitehdas (Cable Factory)

The renovated factory overlooking the western docks, a combination of sights under one roof, houses the following trio of small museums and two dance theatre groups, as well as a restaurant. ⓐ Tallberginkatu 1. ⓣ (09) 4763 8300. ⓦ www.kaapelitehdas.fi Various admission charges. ⓝ Bus/tram 8, 15, 20, 21, 65A or 66A.

Hotel and Restaurant Museum (at Kaapelitehdas) Take a look at Finnish food and drink traditions. ⓣ (09) 6859 3700. ⓦ www.hotellijaravintolamuseo.fi ⓛ Tues–Sun 12.00–19.00.

Finnish Museum of Photography (at Kaapelitehdas) This museum explores the history and artistry of photography from 1840 to the present. ⓣ (09) 686 63621, ⓦ www.fmp.fi ⓛ Tues–Sun 11.00–18.00).

Theatre Museum (at Kaapelitehdas) This offers special exhibits on the history and art of the stage, but its primary focus is on interaction, so visitors can play with the exhibits and try their hand at various forms of theatre art. ⓣ (09) 685 09150. ⓦ www.teatterimuseo.fi ⓛ Tues–Sun 12.00–19.00.

Zodiak Centre for New Dance (at Kaapelitehdas) is a repertory company that explores trends in dance though regular performances. ☎ (09) 694 4948. ⓦ www.zodiak.fi

Dance Theatre Hurjaruuth (at Kaapelitehdas) specialises in children's dance performances. ☎ (09) 565 7250. ⓦ www.hurjaruuth.fi

RETAIL THERAPY

The lovely Fredrikinkatu and the streets adjoining it are known for their fashion and interior-decor boutiques. Stroll Bulevardi to browse or buy art and antiques. Forum is the biggest shopping complex in the city centre, with more than 100 shops, facing onto Mannerheimintie (number 20) and filling the entire area between it and Yrjönkatu.

Aero Find a piece of vintage Alvar Aalto, or the work of other Finnish designers in this shop that specialises in 1930–1970 Finnish design and furnishings. ➌ Yrjönkatu 8. ☎ (09) 680 2185. ⓦ www.aerodesignfurniture.fi

Antik Bulevard It won't be cheap, but it will be good if you find it in this high-class antiquerie. Hours are eccentric, so call or just stop in if it's open. ➌ Bulevardi 5. ☎ (09) 647 286.

Eero Elo Clothing for men and women, from leather skirts to jeans. ➌ Bulevardi 6. ☎ (09) 649 232. ◷ Mon–Fri 10.00–17.00, Sat 10.00–15.00. Ⓝ Tram 6.

Galerie 1900 If you fall in love with the hot-again look of art nouveau while you're in Helsinki, you can take home a piece of the real thing. The shop offers lighting fixtures and decor items in Jugendstil and art deco style. 🅐 Annankatu 11. 🅣 (09) 649 152.

Hietalahti Flea Market Be prepared to bargain for everything from price-off clothes to antiques. The latter may include the family treasures of someone settling an estate or just cleaning house, as well as regular dealers. 🅐 Hietalahdentori. 🅛 Mon–Fri 08.00–14.00, Sat 08.00–15.00.

Hietalahti Market Hall Architect Selim Lindqvist's historic building, across the square from the flea market, is filled with shops and stalls selling local handicrafts, plus cafés. 🅐 Hietalahdentori. 🅛 Mon–Sat 07.00–14.00. 🅝 Tram/bus 8 or 15

Ivana Helsinki Campus Visionary stylish clothes for an easy lifestyle, Ivana's clothes are rich in outdoor themes and designed to be lived in. 🅐 Uudenmaankatu 15. 🅣 (09) 622 4422. 🅦 www.ivanahelsinki.com 🅛 Mon–Fri 11.00–19.00, Sat 11.00–16.00. 🅝 Tram 6.

Le Slip Shop for undergarments at uber-prices, all from the best designers. 🅐 Annankatu 6. 🅣 (09) 640 762. 🅛 Mon–Fri 10.00–17.30, Sat 10.00–14.00.

Limbo Shop Limbo's easy styles flow with the season, from comfortable sundresses in cheery colours to sweats and tee-shirts with a sense of humour. Hip clothes don't get more comfortable. 🅐 Annankatu 13. 🅣 (09) 644 060. 🅦 www.limbo.fi

Lux Shop This shop sells one-of-a-kind fashions by creative young designers, including the fashion pieces rich in printing, embroidery and applique by Rinne Niinikoski. Ⓐ Uudenmaankatu 26. ☎ (09) 678 538. Ⓦ www.lux-shop.com. 🕐 Mon–Sat 12.00–18.00. Ⓝ Tram 6.

Myymala2 A plain-jane environment where young artists can show their work, Myymala2 has launched several talents, as well as creating a venue for gallery-goers. The boutique is a gold-mine of groovy gifts and funky finds. Ⓐ Uudenmaankatu 23. ☎ (041) 7832 327. Ⓦ www.myymala2.com 🕐 Tues–Sun 12.00–18.00. Ⓝ Tram 6.

Nectarine This shoes and clothes boutique for women has a large variety and reasonable prices. There is designer wear, too, but the main emphasis is on the affordable. Ⓐ Iso Roobertinkatu 8. ☎ (09) 642 455. 🕐 Mon–Fri 10.00–18.00, Sat 10.00–15.00. Ⓝ Tram 6.

Popparienkeli Whatever you need in new or used CD singles (especially from the 50s and 60s), you're likely to find it here, along with some vinyl. But ask, since not everything is displayed. Look for other music shops in this vicinity. Ⓐ Fredrikinkatu 12. ☎ (09) 661 638, Ⓦ www.popangel.fi 🕐 Mon–Fri 10.00–18.00, Sat 10.00–16.00. Ⓝ Tram 6.

Stupido Shop If it's on DVD, tape, CD or vinyl, and it's alternative, from humppa to the latest Aavikko, just ask the Stupido guys. Ⓐ Iso Roobertinkatu 20–22. Ⓦ www.stupido.fi 🕐 Mon–Fri 10.00–19.00, Sat 10.00–16.00. Ⓝ Tram 6.

Tiimari The stationery shop we all wish we had in our home town, Tiimari has pens, paper, art supplies, craft materials and projects for all ages. Ⓐ Forum, Yrjönkatu 29. ☎ (09) 694 2773.

Turkisaitta Siperia Furs don't have to be budget-breaking; here you'll find coats under €200, as well as hats and other fur accessories. Or opt for a convincing faux. ➋ Annankatu 11. ➊ (09) 643 641. ⏱ Mon–Fri 10.00–17.00, Sat 10.00–14.00.

TAKING A BREAK

The mega-mall Forum has a number of cafés and small eating places. It's a good rule that wherever shoppers congregate, there will be places to stop for coffee and compare finds.

Café Ekberg Helsinki's oldest café, Ekberg isn't just a period piece, it's a bit of romantic old Europe. Reminiscent of between-the-wars Vienna, it's the kind of place you expect to see writers working on their books.

⊘ *The Finnish motto: when in doubt, have a cup of coffee*

They serve a breakfast buffet, lunch, light meals and tasty pastries or a glass of something in between. ❸ Bulevardi 9. ❶ (09) 605 269. ❶ Mon–Fri 07.30–20.00, Sat 08.30–17.00, Sun 10.00–17.00. ❶ Tram 6.

Café Schubert All ages meet and eat at this comfortable café. Classical daytime music gives way to jazz and other strains at night. ❸ Fredrikinkatu 30. ❶ (09) 694 2887.

Croksu Make yourself at home at one of the café tables to enjoy your soup, pasta or bakery choice, or get another 10 per cent taken off the price of the already inexpensive meals if you choose take-away. ❸ Fredrikinkatu 23. ❶ (09) 680 2850. ❶ Mon–Fri 09.30–16.30.

O'Malley's A Finnish take on an Irish pub, but a good stop for a pint if you're over 20. ❸ Sokos Hotel, Yrjonkatu 26. ❶ (09) 4336 6330. ❶ Mon & Tues 16.00–01.00, Wed & Thur 12.00–01.00, Fri & Sat 12.00–02.00, Sun 18.00–01.00.

Tin Tin Tango Something for everyone in this combination bar, self-serve laudromat, art gallery and sauna in the Töölö neighbourhood. ❸ Töölöntorinkatu 7. ❶ (09) 2709 0972. ❶ Mon–Fri 07.00–02.00, Sat & Sun 10.00–02.00.

AFTER DARK

Along with having some of the hottest clubs and entertainment venues in the city, the neighbourhoods away from the Esplanadi are also the 'low rent district' for bars and pubs. Iso Roobertinkatu is known for its restaurants, pubs and bars, which fill almost the entire street. While a number of places have age limits that cut out those below 20 or 24, most of the places around the Kaampi metro station do not, so traditionally, this is where the under-20s hang out.

Restaurants

Bar Tapasta €€ Tapas, sangria and designer beers are served in a small space, but that doesn't deter the hip followers, who still find it simpatico, however crowded. 🅐 Uudenmaankatu 13. 🕿 (09) 640 724.

Helmi €€–€€€ The stylish decor sets the tone for equally well designed dishes. The inspiration is global and eclectic, and the vegetarian dishes are as well planned and original as the other choices – taro chips and mushroom mousse might accompany a tofu steak. Even the plain-sounding dish of chicken and vegetables is a winner. Minimum age is 24. 🅐 Eerikinkatu 14. 🕿 (09) 612 6410. 🕒 Tues–Thur 17.00–24.00, Fri & Sat 17.00–04.00.

Lappi €€–€€€ Not just Finnish, but only those dishes originating in Lapland are the speciality of this cosy restaurant. Reindeer and other game meats are featured, along with salmon in several forms and boutique farm-made cheeses. The authentic atmosphere of natural wood furnishings and soft lighting is pleasant, too. 🅐 Annankatu 22. 🕿 (09) 645 550.

Lehtovaara €€–€€€ The menu speaks for itself at this exceptional restaurant near the Sibelius Park: fillet of beef with deep-fried garlic potatoes, garlic butter and fried fresh mushroom slices, lightly smoked Arctic char with lobster ravioli or snowgrouse breast with a cake of root vegetables and potato . Vegetarians might be offered cheese polenta with ginger-braised vegetables. 🅐 Mechelininkatu 39. 🕿 (09) 440 833. 🕒 Mon–Fri 11.00–24.00, Sat 16.00–24.00, Sun 13.00–21.00.

Talon Tapaan €€–€€€ Finnish specialties fill the menu, which offers reindeer, rabbit, *blinis* and seafood, along with a fair selection of vegetarian main courses. 🅐 Salomonkatu 19. 🕿 (09) 685 6606. 🕒 Mon–Fri 11.00–24.00, Sat 15.00–24.00.

Farouge €€€ For a change of pace, forsake Nordic for Lebanese to find ingredients such as pistachio nuts and limes with the meats and seafood. 🅐 Yrjönkatu 6. 🕿 (09) 612 3455. 🕒 Mon–Fri 11.00–24.00, Sat 16.00–24.00.

Ravintola Carelia €€€ The wine list alone is staggering, with over 300 varieties, including 50 different champagnes, making it a good place to stop before or after the opera, just across the street. Menu choices are just as difficult. Begin maybe with cep soup with thyme foam, then go on to guinea fowl breast with truffle risotto and bacon. 🅐 Mannerheimintie 56. 🕿 (09) 2709 0976. 🕒 Mon–Fri 11.00–01.00, Sat 16.00–01.00.

Entertainment
Tennispalatsi The indoor tennis stadium was built in 1938 for the Olympics that never happened, but the Finns have put it to good use as a sports area and entertainment venue. One of its 14 cinema screens is northern Europe's largest. Look here, too, for cafés and restaurants. 🅐 Salomonkatu 15. 🕒 (Box office) daily from 10.00.

Bars & clubs
Corona Bar Run by film-director Aki Kaurismaki, this funky bar offers snooker along with Finnish beers, but most of the youngish crowd come for the beer and bar scene, not billiards. 🅐 Eerikinkatu 11. 🕿 (09) 642 002. 🕒 Daily 11.00–02.00. 🚊 Tram 1.

DTM No one has disputed DTM's claim to be the biggest combo of gay café, bar, disco and night club in Scandinavia. Taking it from the top, the upstairs has a cruise ship-style dance floor with disco and traditional dance music on Friday and Saturday. The street level is a café, with internet access. Downstairs, the nightclub has live music, dance and shows, with a killer sound system and over-the-top lighting and video tech. Special nights bring from top drag shows, bubbling foam parties and more. Minimum age 18 between 18.00 and 21.00; after 21.00 it's 24. ❸ Iso Roobertinkatu 28. ❶ (09) 676 314. ⓦ www.dtm.fi ◐ Mon–Sat 09.00–04.00, Sun 12.00–04.00. Admission charge Sat from 24.00. ◓ Tram 3B, 3T.

Highlight Café The building has come a long way from a 1878 church to a raucous big dance floor with three floors of nightclub. The second floor has a full view of the centre stage and dance floor. The music mix appeals to a lot of people, so expect a queue. One of the few large, popular clubs that admit guests at age 18. ❸ Fredrikinkatu 42. ❶ (09) 734 5822, ⓦ www.ravintolahighlight.com ◐ Go between 21.00 and 22.00 Fri or Sat or anytime Wed for free admission.

Lost and Found Gay, straight, whatever. Everyone is welcome and feels at home in this modern restaurant/club/bar/disco. Call it Lostari, to feel like a local. Best to go early, since queues form on the big party nights – Wednesday, Friday, Saturday – before midnight. Age 22 and over. ❸ Annankatu 6. ❶ (09) 680 1010. ⓦ www.lostandfound.fi ◐ Sun–Thur 16.00–04.00, Fri & Sat 15.00–04.00.

Mocambo You name the beat and you'll hear it at Mocambo: dance-hall, hip-hop, funk, R&B, Latin. And you'll meet interesting people,

too, from models to moguls, most in the under-40 set.
ⓐ Ratakatu 9. ☏ (09) 6227 1590.

Onnela Big disco, table-dancing and a section for metal, this place is especially popular because the €5 membership card buys you beers for €1 from 23.00 to 01.00 most nights. ⓐ Fredrikinkatu 48. ⓦ www.ravintolaonnela.fi ⏰ Mon–Wed 23.00–04.00, Thur–Sat 22.00–04.00, Sun 23.00–04.00.

Rose Garden When the others close, everyone heads to this underground club/restaurant for groove, soul, hip-hop, techno and house by DJs and name guest performers. Three bars, two dance floors, one cool place to be. ⓐ Iso-Roobertinkatu 10. ☏ (09) 678 010. ⓦ www.clubrosegarden.com ⏰ Tues–Sat.

Soda It's far from the new kid on the block, but still popular even if its lost its edge with the super-trendies. The daytime coffee bar livens up on weekend nights, with funk, groove, house and techno music, but only for those over 20. ⓐ Uudenmaankatu 16–20. ☏ (09) 612 1012.

Storeyville The city's premier jazz club, Storeyville offers live jazz in an environment that favours listening to the New Orleans-style music and enjoying a drink. The pub upstairs provides a place to wait for the crowd to thin on weekends. ⓐ Museokatu 8. ☏ (09) 408 007. ⏰ Daily 20.00–04.00. Modest admission charge.

Tiger If you want to go where the other tourists go, go here. The Euro-techno scene is so classic as to be a parody of itself. ⓐ Yrjönkatu 36. ☏ (09) 0565 7800.

The islands & outskirts

Helsinki sits in an archipelago, and some of its most outstanding
attractions are on the islands, including the excellent zoo, an
outdoor historical museum and the World Heritage site of
Suomenlinna Fortress. Fortunately, getting to them is quite easy,
thanks to boat and bus services. The ferries to these islands make
inexpensive boat excursions, and are covered by the Helsinki Card
(see page 57).

SIGHTS & ATTRACTIONS

Perhaps Helsinki's foremost place to visit is the island fortress of
Suomenlinna and the museums, craft studios, restaurants and cliff-
edged island itself. Animal lovers will enjoy the zoo, where rare
animals have plenty of room to roam. Between the ferries and
various excursion boats, there are several ways to view the city from
the water and to explore the archipelago.

Boat trips

You can enjoy the views of elegant Helsinki and get a cheap mini-
cruise, by taking any of the several ferries that shuttle between
Market Square and the islands of Suomenlinna and Korkeasaari,
where the zoo is located.

 The ferry to Korkeasaari continues on to Hakaniemenranta quay
in the Kallio neighbourhood behind the railway station, where there
is another daily market. Ferries leave Market Square for
Suomenlinna daily 06.00–02.20, and Katajanokka (east of Market
Square and the harbour) Mon–Fri 07.25–15.25. Another ferry leaves
from the southern tip of the city, in the Eira neighbourhood, bound

for Pihlajasaari, a beach-ringed island west of Suomenlinna.
🕿 (09) 010 0111.

A number of traditional cruises ply the waters around Helsinki. Sun Lines explores the tree-lined Degerö Canal, Korkeasaari zoo, the Finnish icebreakers and the cruise ship harbours, along with circling Suomenlinna sea fortress, in comfortable cruisers that offer a coffee and drink bar. 🕿 (020) 741 8210. ⓦ www.sunlines.fi 🕒 May–Sept.

IHA lines offer à la carte dining on their boats as they cruise through the archipelago on trips that last from 90 minutes to 3 hours. Three different routes, each beginning at Market Square, cover the eastern islands or the fortress and surrounding islands. Booking is essential for dining cruises. 🕿 (09) 6874 5050. ⓦ www.ihalines.fi 🕒 May–Sept.

◗ *Escape from the city to the tranquility of the forested islands*

Along with archipelago cruises, Royal Lines offers daily trips to the medieval town of Porvoo in July and August (see page 124).

Suomenlinna Fortress

One of the world's largest sea fortresses, the 18th-century fort on Suomenlinna has a fascinating past and an interesting present. A 15-minute ferry ride from Market Square brings you to the group of connected islands, where there is enough to occupy an entire day – and in the summer, an evening, too. It was built in 1847 by the Swedes, who owned Finland then, to scare off the Russians, who eventually captured both it and Finland, turning the island's guns figuratively to the west. The impressive fortifications became a UNESCO World Heritage Site in 1991.

In the visitor centre a wide screen show, 'The Suomenlinna Experience', explores the fortress's long history, in English. Sign up

here for guided walks that help bring all the sites into a whole picture. In the same building is the museum, which gives a picture of how officers and soldiers lived during the Swedish and Russian rules. The fortress was also used by the Finns after independence as a prison for Communist detainees, a military garrison, a submarine base and the Valmet shipyard, which made ships as reparations for the Soviet Union after World War II.

Walking and cycling paths (you must bring cycles from the mainland as none are hired here) lead along the cliffs and to small beaches. Be careful on the cliff paths, since these are not fenced, and when on the beaches with children, because of dangerous sudden ship wakes and currents. Various buildings house studios and shops of glassblowers, potters and other craftsmen.

(i) (09) 684 1880. **(L)** Daily 10.00–16.00. Admission charge. **(N)** Ferries leave Market Square for Suomenlinna daily 06.00–02.20. Boats also leave Katajanokka (beyond Uspensky Cathedral) Mon–Fri 07.25–15.25. **(i)** (09) 010 0111.

Ehrensvärd Museum

The museum, in the former home of the fort's designer and commander Augustin Ehrensvärd, depicts the earliest Swedish period with models, arms, furniture and paintings. The Doll and Toy Museum displays dolls, dollhouses, teddy bears and other toys from 1830 to the present, set in an old Russian villa, well worth seeing in its own right. The 250-ton submarine *Vesikko* was commissioned by the German Navy, but was used by the Finnish Navy from 1936 until the end of World War II.

(a) Suomenlinna Fortress. **(L)** Daily. 10.00–17.00 mid-May–Aug; 11.00–15.00 Sept.

Doll and Toy Museum (i) (09) 668.417. **(L)** Sat & Sun 11.00–16.00.

Seurasaari Open-air Museum

Historic buildings from all parts of Finland have been rescued and moved to this outdoor museum, beautifully insulated from Helsinki's busy 21st-century world on its own island. The village of 87 buildings centres around the farmstead, a working farm where livestock and crops are raised using old methods. Grander by far is the 18th-century Kahiluoto manor house, with its well-preserved interior, and the parsonage from Iisalmi. The oldest building preserved here is the wooden Karuna church from the 1600s. A regular series of workshops and programmes highlight folk life and traditional skills for visitors.

❶ (09) 4050 9660 (summer); (09) 4050 9327 (winter). **❷** Mon–Fri 09.00–15.00, Sat & Sun 11.00–17.00 late May & early Sept; daily 11.00–17.00 (until 19.00 Wed) June–Aug; Sat & Sun 11.00–17.00 mid-Sept–late Nov. Admission charge. **❷** Bus 24.

Kekkonen Museum

The home of Finland's most famous president, Urho Kekkonen, is a fine villa set in a park estate adjacent to the island of Seurasaari. Tamminiemi Villa was his official residence during his presidency, from 1956 to 1981. The villa is furnished with outstanding examples of Finnish design and art, as well as gifts of state. In the summer, the tour included the sauna, which was the scene of a number of high-level meetings between Soviet and Western diplomats during the Cold War. **ⓐ** Seurasaarentie 15. **❶** (09) 4050 9650. **ⓦ** www.nba.fi **❷** Daily 11.00–17.00 mid-May–mid-Aug; Thur–Sun 11.00–17.00 mid-Aug–mid-May. Admission charge. **❷** Bus 24.

Korkeasaari Zoo

More than just a place for visitors to view exotic wildlife, Helsinki's zoo is a well respected leader in the preservation and breeding of endangered species. Their snow leopard successes are legendary in zoo annals, and they continue to have rare species of the big cats. Currently these include, in addition to the snow leopards, Amur tiger, Siberian tiger, of which there are only a few hundred remaining, and the exceedingly rare Asian lion from India. Rare Arctic species include the polar fox and musk ox, whose protection from icy winters includes hair a metre (3 ft) long. Environments represented include tropical rainforests to arctic tundra, and the collections include 200 species of animals, with 1000 species of plants to make them feel at home. Founded in 1889, it is one of the oldest zoos in the world.

🄰 Korkeasaari. 🕿 (09) 169 5969 🆆 www.zoo.hel.fi. 🕐 Daily 10.00–20.00 May–Sept; 10.00–16.00 Oct–Feb; 10.00–18.00 Mar–Apr. Admission charge. 🄽 Ferry daily from Market Square or Hakaniemi Market May–Sept; Bus 11 summer and winter weekends; on winter weekdays, bus 16 or metro to Kulosaari, then a 1.5 km (1 mile) walk.

Hvitträsk

If the artistic buzz of the Arts & Crafts and art nouveau period fires your imagination, it's worth the 30 km (18 mile) bus ride to visit the local shrine to this style, built as home and studio to some of its most illustrious lights. Designed by architects Herman Gesellius, Armas Lindgren and Eliel Saarinen, the log-and-stone home is the epitome of the National Romantic style. The architects all lived and worked there at some point, and it was here that the plans were drawn for the Helsinki Railway Station and others of the firm's most famous works. This was the boyhood home of Eliel's son, Eero Saarinen, known for designing American buildings and monuments such as the Gateway Arch in St Louis, Missouri.

ⓐ Hvitträskintie 166, Luoma. ❶ (09) 4050 9630. ⓦ www.nba.fi
🕙 Daily 11.00–18.00 Apr–Oct; Tues–Sun 11.00–17.00 Nov–Mar.
Admission charge. Ⓝ From Kamppi bus terminal, platform 55, take
bus 166, which terminates at Hvitträsk.

Uunisaari Island

Just off the southern tip of the city and reached by boat from
Kompassitorilta (mid-April–mid-Nov) and Ponttoonisilta (mid-
Nov–mid-Apr), both near Kaivopuisto park, Uunisaari offers sand
beaches with lifeguards, café, restaurant and sauna. The well
protected beach is a good one for children.
❶ (09) 636 870. ⓦ www.uunisaari.com

Pihlajasaari Island

To get away from it all and luxuriate in the sun on an island in the
Gulf of Finland, take the boat to the rocks and beaches of
Pihlajasaari. Rent a private changing cabin or bare it all on the
nudist beach. (You'll need clothes for the café, and for the boat ride!)
ⓦ www.jt-line.fi 🕙 May–Sept. Ⓝ Boats depart Meriasatamanranta.

CULTURE

Didrichsen Art Museum

A couple's private collection is now a museum rich in 20th-century
art, along with specialised collections of Asian antiquities of the
Shang and Ming dynasties and pre-Columbian art of the Olmec,
Jalisco and Mayan cultures. Primary here is the Finnish art from the
20th century, including works by Edelfelt and his contemporaries.
Non-Finnish modern art includes works by Picasso, Kandinsky and
Miro.

ⓐ Kuusilahdenkuja 1, Kuusisaari. ☎ (09) 477 8330.
ⓦ www.didrichsenmuseum.fi ⏱ Tues, Thur–Sun 11.00–18.00, Wed
11.00– 20.00, Sept–May. Admission charge. 🚌 Bus 194, 195 from
Elielsquare (platform 25), and 503-506.

Arabia Museum

The Arabia company began in 1874, and moved into the design of
modern tableware in the 1930s. But it was not until the 1960s that it
became a worldwide name in smart dinnerware and porcelain
design. Follow the history of this well known company, along with
the development of Finnish and modern design in home furnishings
in the museum, where 1600 examples of utility and decorative
porcelain from the past 125 years are shown. You'll also find the
company's factory outlet shop here, with excellent bargains on
imperfect and overstocked items.
ⓐ Hämeentie 135. ☎ (09) 204 3910. ⓦ www.arabia.fi ⏱ Tues–Fri
12.00–18.00, Sat & Sun 10.00–16.00. 🚊 Tram/bus 6, 52, 68, 71,71V, 73B,
74, 77S, 503 or 735K.

Gallen-Kallela Museum

The most important Finnish artist of the early 1900s, Gallen-Kallela
had a rich and varied career in painting, drawing, graphics,
sculpture, posters, photographs and applied art, all of which are
represented in this museum. It also tells about the artist's colourful
life and times, as well as his friends. Gallen-Kallela designed this
Jugendstil home and studio, built 1911–1913. The wooden Tarvaspää
villa, built in the 1850s, houses a café.
ⓐ Gallen-Kallelantie 27, Espoo. ☎ (09) 541 3388. ⓦ www.gallen-
kallela.fi ⏱ Daily 10.00–18.00 mid-May–Aug; Tues–Sat 10.00–16.00,
Sun 10.00–17.00 Sept–mid-May. Admission charge. 🚊 Tram 4 to

Munkkiniemi, at Laajalahden aukio, then walk 2 km (1½ miles)
through Munkinpuisto Park (Mon–Fri bus service from
Munkkiniemen puistotie).

RETAIL THERAPY

Outside the busy and trendy shopping streets of downtown
Helsinki, the islands and outer suburbs nonetheless offer some
quality shopping. The fortress of Suomenlinna houses a number of
excellent artisan studios, and museum shops offer unique speciality
gifts. And Arabia's factory outlet is a mecca for bargain hunters with
a taste for fine dinnerware.

Arabia Factory Shop One of Scandinavia's best-known brands of
porcelain and dinnerware, Arabia spans all ages and tastes with its
classic lines and functional style. The outlet offers discontinued
styles and seconds at deep discounts. Along with the Arabia label
are goods in Iittala and other company brands. See page opposite
for access details.

Arts and Crafts Summer Shop Selected traditional and modern
crafts in all media. ⓐ Suomenlinna B 34. ⓣ (050) 408 2902.
ⓛ Daily 11.00–20.00 mid-May–Sept.

Goldsmith Timo Mustajärvi Studio producing gold jewellery.
ⓐ Bastion Hårleman, Suomenlinna. ⓛ Mon–Fri 10.30–15.00 June;
Mon–Thur 10.30–18.00 July.

Hvitträsk Museum Shop A source of the beautiful Kalevala and
Kaunis *koru* jewellery, based on designs from Finnish folklore, this

outstanding museum gift shop also carries art and architecture books and prints, and crafts made by the Friends of Finnish Handicrafts. The work of local artists includes art glass, jewellery, ceramics, sculpture, knitted woollens and linen tablecloths.
🅰 Hvitträskintie 166, Luoma. 🕿 (09) 4050 .9630. Ⓦ www.nba.fi

Jetty Barracks Gallery Operated by the Helsinki Artists' Association, the gallery shows exhibitions of juried contemporary art in the rooms of the Jetty Barracks. 🅰 Iso Mustasaari, next to the Main

🔽 *Traditional handicrafts are always high-quality, if sometimes unbearably cute*

Quay, Suomenlinna. ☏ (09) 673 140. 🕐 Tues–Thur 12.30–18.00,
Fri–Sun 11.30–16.00.

Pot Viapori Ceramics Studio ❷ Suomenlinna B 45. ☏ (09) 668 151.
🕐 Daily 11.00–18.00 mid-July–late Aug.

Safari Shop The Korkeasaari Zoo's own brand of animal-themed and
environmentally friendly products, as well as Fair Trade products and
crafts from cooperatives in developing countries, are sold in the
zoo's shop. ❸ Korkeasaari. ☏ (09) 696 2370. 🕐 Daily. 10.00–20.00
May–Sept; 10.00–16.00 Oct–Feb; 10.00–18.00 Mar–Apr.

Seurasaari Museum Shop Traditional Finnish handicrafts, authentic
sauna products, books and other historical items are available in the
museum store. ❷ Seurasaari. ☏ (09) 4050 9662. 🕐 Daily 11.00–17.00
June–Aug; Mon–Fri 09.00–15.00, Sat & Sun 11.00–17.00, late May &
early Sept.

TAKING A BREAK

Nearly every museum has its own café, usually open at least the
same hours as the museum itself. Suomenlinna is well supplied
with eating places, several of which are listed under 'After Dark'
below, since they are open for evening meals, as well. For travel
directions, see under the corresponding museum or attraction.

Café Antin Kaffeliiteri In a little shed building next to Antti
farmstead, the café bakes traditional Finnish pastries and otherwise
hard-to-find old-fashioned regional treats, including Karelian rice
pastries and pancakes from the Aland Islands. The cinnamon rolls

are addictive. ⓐ Seurasaari. ⓣ (09) 4050 9660. ⓛ Daily 11.00–17.00
June–Aug; Mon–Fri 09.00–15.00, Sat & Sun 11.00–17.00 late May
and early Sept.

Café Bar Valimo The grass-roofed ammunition foundry that houses
this summer café is located on the docks near an old wooden sailing
vessel and the guest harbour. Valimo serves soups, pasta dishes,
snacks, sandwiches and soft drinks, as well as having a full alcohol
licence. ⓐ Building B 13, Suomenlinna. ⓣ (09) 692 6450.
ⓦ www.valimo.org ⓛ Mon–Thur 11.00–20.30, Fri & Sat 11.00–22.30,
Sun 11.00–18.30 May–mid-June; Mon–Sat 10.30–22.30, Sun
10.30–20.30 mid-June–mid-Aug. Closes earlier late Aug.

Café Piper In a charming old wooden villa set in a park, with a
terrace overlooking the sea, Café Piper serves soup, savoury snacks,
pastries and drinks including beer. ⓐ Building B56, Suomenlinna.
ⓣ (09) 668 447. ⓛ Daily. 10.00–17.00 May; 10.00–19.00 June–mid-
Aug; 10.00–17.00 mid-Aug–mid-Sept.

Café Vanille Opposite the church in the Russian merchants' quarter,
cosy modern Café Vanille serves soups and sandwiches, along with
fresh-baked pastries, cappuccino, tea, hot cocoa and beer.
ⓐ Building C18, Suomenlinna. ⓣ (040) 556 1169. ⓛ Fri–Sun
11.00–17.00 May; Daily 11.00–18.00 June–Sept; Wed–Fri 11.00–16.00,
Sat 11.00–18.00, Sun 11.00–17.00 Oct; Sat 11.00–17.00, Sun
12.00–17.00 Nov–Dec.

Hvitträsk Located in the estate's Little Villa, the Café Hvitträsk offers
sandwiches and pastries, coffee, tea and alcoholic drinks in a
charming atmosphere. On the second floor of the villa, the

upmarket restaurant has a terrace for summer dining. An à la carte menu is offered in the evening. ❷ Hvitträsk, Hvitträskintie 166, Luoma. ❶ (09) 297 6033. ❸ Café: daily 11.00–18.00. Restaurant: Mon–Sat 11.30–23.00, Sun 11.30–22.00.

Korkeasaari Zoo A variety of kiosks and cafés serve snacks and lunches in the summer, including Café Coco and kiosks by the Bear Castle and Café Safari near the Mustikkamaa entrance.

Pizzeria Nikolai Inside the stone casemates of the fortress at King's gate, Nikolai serves good pizza. In the summer, you can enjoy it on the terrace with a sea view. The waterbus goes directly to King's Gate, or you can take the ferry and stop here on your walk around the connecting islands. ❷ Building A7, King's Gate, Suomenlinna. ❶ (09) 668 552. ❸ Sat 12.00–22.00, Sun 12.00–20.00 early May; Sun–Thur 12.00–20.00, Fri & Sat 12.00–22.00 mid-May–Aug.

Pukki Restaurant Serving meals and hot snacks in the daytime, Pukki also offers an à la carte dinner menu and live music some summer evenings 19.00–24.00. ❷ Korkeasaari Zoo. ❶ (09) 2705 1150. ❸ Year-round.

Restaurant Café Chapman Near the Visitor Centre, the year-round café with a courtyard terrace is a lunch spot, and summer evenings an à la carte restaurant. ❷ Building B1, Suomenlinna. ❶ (09) 668 692. ❸ Mon–Fri 10.30–15.00 Jan–early May; Mon–Fri 11.00–21.00, Sat 12.00–21.00, Sun 12.00–18.00 late May–mid-Sept; Mon–Fri 10.30–15.00 mid-Sept–Dec.

Seurasaari Several historic kiosks serve food and offer tables for

those with picnics. The kiosk by the bridge (🕐 Daily 11.00–16.00
June–Aug) used to be in central Helsinki, and the Kiosk in the
Festival Grounds (🕐 Sat & Sun 11.00–16.00) has a grill available for
barbecue. ☎ (09) 484 511.

Tarvaspää The villa was Gallen-Kallela's summer house until 1913,
when the studio was completed. The caféteria is now there, serving
traditional fresh-baked Finnish pastries, including cinnamon buns,
called *korvapuusti*. 🄰 Gallen-Kallelantie 27, Espoo. ☎ (09) 541 3388.
🆆 www.gallen-kallela.fi 🕐 Tues–Thur 10.00–20.00, Fri–Mon
10.00–18.00 mid-May–Aug; Tues–Sat 10.00–16.00, Sun 10.00–17.00
Sept–mid-May.

Toy Museum Café Tucked into the wooden Russian villa with the Toy
Museum, this cosy tearoom and terrace serves Russian-style tea,
real lemonade and fresh-baked pastries, including wonderful apple
pie. 🄰 Building C66, Suomenlinna. ☎ (09) 668 417. 🕐 Sat & Sun
11.00–16.00 Apr; daily 11.00–16.00 late May; daily 11.00–17.00 June;
daily 11.00–18.00 July; daily 11.00–17.00 Aug; Sat & Sun 11.00–16.00
Sept.

AFTER DARK

Apart from the islands of Suomenlinna, most of the 'museum
islands' are daytime destinations. One or two restaurants might
offer evening meals, but the city's nightlife is centred in its in-town
neighbourhoods. That said, if you plan to be at one of the outlying
museums, such as Hvitträsk, in the late afternoon, their restaurants
are well worth considering for their charm and their unhurried
ambience.

Restaurants

Suomenlinna Petty Officers' Club €–€€ Not fancy, but a favourite place for locals to meet, the club is in one of the old wooden buildings near the ferry landing. The terrace overlooks the city, across the water. ⓐ Building C8, Suomenlinna. ☎ (09) 668 273. 🕐 Mon–Fri 16.00–22.45, Sat 12.00–22.45, Sun 12.00–18.45, Jan–mid-Dec.

Suomenlinna Panimo Brewery Restaurant €€ The brewery, brewpub and restaurant are inside the high-vaulted casements of the Jetty Barracks, built during the Russian control of the fort. Sample the brewery's own Höpken Pils, Coyet Ale and the dark Helsinki Portteri. Booking is wise in the summer. ⓐ Building C1, Suomenlinna. ☎ (09) 228 5030. 🕐 Wed–Fri 15.00–22.00, Sat 12.00–22.00, Sun 12.00–18.00 Jan–Mar; Mon–Fri 15.00–22.00, Sat 12.00–22.00, Sun 12.00–18.00 Apr; Mon–Sat 11.00–23.30, Sun 12.00–18.00 May–Aug; Mon–Fri 15.00–22.00, Sat 12.00–22.00, Sun 12.00–18.00 Sept–Dec.

Helsinki by Sea Dinner Cruise €€–€€€ Enjoy a changing land and seascape over dinner on board a sightseeing boat with a full kitchen. The à la carte menu offers starters such as forest mushroom cream soup or salmon soup, and main courses like grilled breast of chicken in a gorgonzola sauce. Book in advance for these popular evening excursions. IHA Lines. ☎ (09) 6874 5050. 🌐 www.ihalines.fi 🕐 Tues–Sat 19.00 May–Sept.

Restaurant Särkänlinna €€€ On the island of Särkkä between Suomenlinna and the southern tip of the city, the summer restaurant in a stone fortress offers stunning sea views and a setting rich in history. If you think the floor of the long dining room tilts a bit, you're right; it was designed to make it easier to get cannonballs to the cannons at the far end. ⓐ Särkkä. ⓣ (09) 134 561. ⓦ www.palace.fi ⓛ Mon–Sat 17.30–24.00 May–Sept. ⓝ Reached by ferry from the Ullanlinna quay on the mainland at the southern end of the city.

Walhalla Restaurant €€€ King's Gate is at the far end of the small island of Kustaanmiekka, attached to Suomenlinna, and Walhalla is set in the stone-arched interior of the fortress there. It's worth the waterbus ride – an enjoyable evening trip – to savour such starters as mousse of smoked Arctic char with whitebait roe, or main courses such as fillet of reindeer with morel sauce. You can end a meal with equally traditional local ingredients: try cloudberry charlotte with cloudberry melba. The views from the terrace bar are just as outstanding. Be sure to book ahead. ⓐ Building A7, King's Gate, Suomenlinna. ⓣ (09) 668 552. ⓦ www.restaurantwalhalla.com ⓛ Sun–Thur 12.00–20.00, Fri & Sat 12.00–22.00 May–mid-Sept.

Entertainment
Suomenlinna Summer Theatre Productions are in Finnish, but the programme is based on movement, action, dance and music, so the words are not essential to enjoying the performance. These take place on both Suomenlinna and Seurasaari islands. Tickets from Lippupalvelu, Stockmann Department Store or Sokos Department Store. ⓣ 0600 108 00. ⓦ www.lippupalvelu.fi ⓛ June–Aug.

ⓞ *The forbidding keep of Finland's largest castle is one of the sights of Turku*

OUT OF TOWN
trips

Porvoo

Dating from the 1500s, Porvoo is Finland's second-oldest town, and lies 50 km (30 miles) east of Helsinki. Today the town is known for its small shops specialising in crafts and antiques, enough reason for a day trip here. Along with a day cruise, trains and buses also connect Porvoo to Helsinki. Royal Lines offers daily trips to Poorvoo in July and August. Departing Market Square at 10.00 the cruise goes through the archipelago while guests enjoy lunch on board. After travelling up the river past the colourful old town, with its riverside storehouses, there are about two hours to explore the town's cathedral, wooden buildings and narrow lanes lined with shops and cafés, before the return voyage to Helsinki.

Porvoo Tourist Office ⓐ Rihkamakatu 4. ① (019) 520 2316.
ⓦ www.porvoo.fi ⓛ Mon–Fri 09.00–18.00, Sat & Sun 10.00–16.00
June–Aug; Mon–Fri 09.30–16.30, Sat 10.00–14.00 Sept–Jan.
Royal Lines ① (09) 612 2950. ⓦ www.royalline.fi ⓛ Mid-May–mid-Sept.

SIGHTS & ATTRACTIONS

Porvoo's picturesque riverfront is lined with little red wooden

● *Porvoo's many boutiques make it a popular day-trip destination*

buildings that were once storehouses for the city's mercantile trade. The land rises from these to the old town, a charming tangle of old streets lined with ochre-coloured wooden houses in typically Karielian architecture. Two museums face the market square of the old town, one with historical collections and the other an art museum featuring the work of several art nouveau-era artists.

Cathedral

Topping the hill is the cathedral, parts of which date from the 14th century, although it was largely reconstructed a century later and became a cathedral in 1723. Highlights are the ornate 1764 pulpit and wall paintings from the 15th century.

ⓐ Kirkkotori 1. ⓘ (019) 661 11. 🕐 Mon–Fri 10.00–18.00, Sat 10.00–14.00, Sun 14.00–17.00, May–Sept; Tues–Sat 10.00–14.00, Sun 14.00–16.00, Oct–Apr.

Edelfelt-Vallgren Museum

Porvoo is where the artist Louis Sparr founded the Iris Factory, which pioneered furniture and ceramic manufacture in the Arts and Crafts tradition. Also working here was Porvoo native and prominent artist, Albert Edelfelt. Dozens of examples of the Iris Factory ceramics, Sparr's furniture, sculpture of Ville Vallgren and Edelfelt's paintings are displayed in the museum.

ⓐ Valikatu 11. ⓘ (019) 574 7500. 🕐 Mon–Sat 10.00–16.00, Sun 11.00–16.00, May–Aug; Wed–Sun 12.00–16.00, Sept–Apr. Admission charge.

Runeberg Museum

Even before Sparr and Edelfelt made Porvoo into an art colony, it had been a centre of creative talent. Finland's national poet, Johan Ludvig

Runeberg, lived and wrote here for more than two decades from 1852 onwards, drawing other talent of his times to Porvoo. The home has been a museum since 1882. 🄰 Aleksanterinkatu 3. 🕓 (019) 581 330.

TAKING A BREAK

The following represent just a small selection from the wide choice of cafés and restaurants in Porvoo.

Café Fanny Friendly café in an 18th-century building on the Town Hall Square in old Porvoo, serving good coffee and fresh-baked cinnamon buns. 🄰 Välikatu 13. 🕓 (019) 582 855.

Old Town Café Sandwiches and pastries to eat in or take out. 🄰 Välikatu 1. 🕓 (019) 580 201.

Porvoon Paahtimo This red-tiled converted warehouse in the old historic centre of Porvoo is easy to spot. Excellent coffee choice and a river-facing terrace. 🄰 Mannerheiminkatu 2. 🕓 (019) 617 040. 🆆 www.porvoonpaahtimo.fi

ACCOMMODATION

Hotel Seurahovi €€ Centrally located, the modern building offers nicely appointed rooms, saunas, a sports bar and restaurant. Close by the 19th century steam ship *Glickauf* is another dining choice. Rauhankatu 27. 🕓 (019) 547 61. 🕓 (019) 524 9329. 🆆 www.seurahovi.fi

---

🅞 *Porvoo's market is a good place to pick up hand-knitted Finnish woollens*

Turku

Finland's oldest city at almost 800 years old, Turku was the capital until 1812. It is the most traditional medieval town in Finland, with a castle, marketplace, cathedral and a river harbour. In Turku you will see architecture ranging from the 1200s to art nouveau and the stunning modern Sibelius Museum by Woldemar Baeckman. Charming, if quiet, Turku proclaims itself as Finland's Christmas City. Visit then, or during the midsummer Medieval Festival, when the old square regains its medieval air, with craft stalls and food vendors. The Turku Card (€ 21 for 24 hours) gives free admission to all city museums and transport, worthwhile if you plan to see a lot of museums. Frequent trains and buses from Helsinki take about 2 hours to Turku.

Turku Touring Stop here for tourist information and maps of the south-west coast. ⓐ Aurakatu 4. ⓣ (02) 262 7444. ⓦ www.turku.fi ⓛ Mon–Fri 08.30–18.00, Sat & Sun 09.00–16.00 Apr–Sept; Sat & Sun 10.00–15.00 Oct–Mar.

SIGHTS & ATTRACTIONS

The river is alive in summer as historic boats line the shore, ferries cross, families picnic and lovers stroll alongside the water. Music drifts from the restaurant boats and the whole town seems to gather there in the long evenings. In winter, lights fill the trees and reflect off the snow in a glittering fairy-tale world as skaters skim along its frozen surface.

Turku Castle
Built between 1280 and 1650, Finland's largest castle is a defensive

Cathedral

Kuralan
kylämäki

Uudenmaankatu

Old Great Square

Luostarinmäki
Museum

Kaskenkatu

Aboa Vetus &
Ars Nova

Aurakatu

Market Hall

Uimastadion

Urheilupuisto

Bus Station

Eerikinkatu

Linnankatu

Aura

Itäinen Rantakatu

Hämeenkatu

Yliopistonkatu

Itäinen Pitkäkatu

Martinkatu

Koulukatu

Ratapihankatu

Puistokatu

Sairashuoneenkatu

Linnankatu

Läntinen Rantakatu

Läntinen Rantakatu

Sairalininkatu

Moomin World
& Naantali

Pansiontie

Forum Marinum

Turku Castle

500m

N

o

pile with outer walls 3 m (10 ft) thick. Enter its maze of stairways and passages through a picturesque courtyard to find towers, banqueting halls and a chapel with medieval woodcarving. Historical exhibits highlight events, customs and dress.

ⓐ Linnankatu 80. ☏ (02) 262 0300. ⏱ Daily 10.00–18.00 mid-Apr–mid-Sept; Tues–Sun 10.00–15.00 mid-Sept–mid-Apr; Sat 10.00–17.00 Oct–mid-Apr. Admission charge. Ⓝ Bus 1.

Forum Marinum

A combination museum, shipyard and maritime research facility, the Forum includes two buildings (and 3500 exhibits) and two historic vessels to tour, the full-rigger *Suomen Joutsen* and the minelayer *Keihässalmi*. Exhibits feature navy and commercial ships, local coastal boats and culture. A second building contains boats and tools for boatbuilding.

ⓐ Linnankatu 72. ☏ (02) 282 9511. ⓦ www.forum-marinum.fi ⏱ Daily 11.00–19.00 May–Sept; Tues–Sun 10.00–18.00 Oct–Apr. Ships: daily 11.00–19.00 June–Aug. Admission charge. Ⓝ Bus 1.

The Old Great Square

The ensemble of old buildings near the river was the historic centre of power, both church and state, when Turku was the capital. Brinkkala mansion was the residence of the Russian Governor General, and the stables in its courtyard are now artisans' studios. The entire square becomes a marketplace before Christmas and during the Medieval Market from late June to early August.
ⓦ www.keskiaikaisetmarkkinat.fi

Turku Cathedral

In 1229, the Pope ordered a church to be built here, and the cathedral remained Catholic until the mid-16th century, when it became Finland's Lutheran mother church. Burned or pillaged 30 times throughout its history, it has been rebuilt each time, and remains a landmark of Finnish architecture. Although its lines are familiar perpendicular Gothic, the interior is entirely plastered, without visible stonework.

ⓐ Tuomiokirkkotori 20.

Luostarinmäki Handicrafts Museum

An entire neighbourhood of 40 homes, the only ones saved from the fire that destroyed Turku in 1827, is preserved as a museum village, showing how ordinary people lived. Homes and workshops open onto little courtyards, surrounded by stables and small rooms built as families grew. About 30 artisans demonstrate period crafts, from wire weaving and printing to carving shaved-wood ornaments, and you can buy from them or from the shop (see page 136).

ⓐ Luostarinmäki. ⓣ (02) 262 0350. ⓛ Daily 10.00–18.00 mid-Apr–mid-Sept; Tues–Sun 10.00–15.00 mid-Sept–mid-Apr. Admission charge. ⓝ Bus 3, 12,18, 24 or 30.

Kuralan kylämäki (Village of Living History)

A working 1950s farm on the eastern outskirts of city takes visitors back half a century to smell fresh goodies baking in the farmhouse kitchen and pet baby animals in the barns. Hands-on activities bring the farm to life for children, who can make a whistle from a willow stick or play shops using real items from the period. At weekends in December the farm is decorated for the holidays and hosts a craft market, with prices far below those of street markets.

ⓐ Jaanintie 45. ⓣ (02) 262 0420. ⓛ Daily in summer and for special weekend events. ⓝ Bus 28.

Boat trips

Opportunities to explore the River Aura and the archipelago include everything from a free ferry to dinner-dance cruises and day-long sails. The City Ferry (*Föri*) crosses the Aura from early morning until midnight, year round. From June to August the Pikkuföri river ferry plies the river from the Forum Marinum (€2). M/s *Ruissalo* cruises daily June–August between Turku and Ruissalo Island.

Airisto Line Oy ☏ (040) 593 0200.

Moomin World

Finland's most famous cartoon characters, the Moomins, will please even children who did not grow up with their adventures. Moomins cavort in the story settings, such as Moominhouse, Moominpapa´s Boat, Hemulens House and the Witch's Labyrinth. At the Pancake Factory children make their own pancake and choose favourite toppings.

🅐 Naantali. ☏ (02) 511 1111. 🅦 www.muumimaailma.fi
🕓 Daily 10.00–18.00 mid-June–late Aug. Admission charge.

CULTURE

Along with the historic buildings and ships, Turku has three museums well worth seeing. Two of these occupy different levels of the same site.

Aboa Vetus & Ars Nova

Built around an excavated city block of medieval Turku, Aboa Vetus explores not only the history of the site, but the archaeology of its discovery and preservation. The foundations have been dug 7 m (22 ft) deep to disclose glimpses of the medieval town, where artefacts, the stones themselves and exquisite models combine to tell the story. Guided tours are in English, daily July–Aug at 11.30.

Above, in the same building, Ars Nova couldn't be in sharper contrast to the medieval world below. More than 500 works by major contemporary and 20th-century artists from Finland and elsewhere trace movements and styles in modern art.
ⓐ Itäinen Rantakatu 4–6. ① (02) 2500 552.
ⓦ www.aboavetusarsnova.fi ● Daily 11.00–19.00 late Mar–mid-Sept; Tues–Sun 11.00–19.00 Jan–late Mar & mid-Sept–mid-Dec. Admission charge. Ⓝ Bus 13, 30 or 55.

Sibelius Museum

See this for the building, even if Sibelius and music leave you cold. Built in 1968, it was Finland's first glass and concrete building, and the concrete simulates rough-cut wood, its organic sand colour enhanced by lighting. Museum exhibits include rare musical instruments, sheet music and memorabilia, with signage in English. The atrium is a beautiful setting for Wednesday evening concerts.
ⓐ Piispankatu 17. ① (02) 215 4494. ⓦ www.sibeliusmuseum.abo.fi
● Tues–Sun 11.00–16.00, Wed also 18.00–20.00. Admission charge.
Ⓝ Bus 4, 28, 30, 50, 51, 53 or 54.

RETAIL THERAPY

Kiosks in the central square sell fresh produce, sizzling sausages, flowers and crafts, changing with the seasons, from early morning until 18.00 Monday to Friday, until 14.00 on Saturday. Overlooking this is the large Sokos department store (ⓐ Eerikinkatu 11. ① (010) 765 020) and from the square's upper corner runs Kauppiaskatu, the main shopping street. Small shops are scattered through the central

 OUT OF TOWN

streets around the market square and two shopping centres –
Hansa and Forum – are close by.

Antiikkiliike Wanha Elias Shop or browse for antique furniture and
decorator pieces. ⓐ Eerikinkatu 29. ⓣ (040) 084 6817.
ⓦ www.antiikkiliikewanhaelias.fi

Arabia Hackman Iittala Finnish design, from glassware and china to
cooking pots, in a factory outlet store. ⓐ Hämeenkatu 6.
ⓣ (020) 439 3547.

Boreus Everything for the outdoors – fishing gear, all-weather
clothes, boots – as well as everyday wear. ⓐ Eerikinkatu 9.
ⓣ (02) 251 9409.

Christmas Market & Medieval Market The Old Great Square comes
alive with people shopping for crafts and munching hearty
traditional foods in the first three weeks in December and from late
June to early August.

Diamina Oy/Figura Shop Turku Accessorise, accessorise, accessorise!
You'll find everything you need right here. ⓐ Kauppiaskatu 3.
ⓣ (02) 469 1074.

Fatabur The museum shop at Turku Castle sells a well-chosen
selection of tasteful gifts, including historic glassware and jewellery
reproductions, as well as traditional crafts (see 'Sights & Attractions'
for access details).

ⓞ *The atrium of the Sibelius Museum doubles as a concert hall*

Föritupa Traditional and contemporary Finnish crafts.
🅐 Sairashuoneenkatu 1. ☎ (02) 331 073. 🕐 Mon–Fri 10.00–14.00, Thur 10.00–17.30.

Kolme Kolikkoa Decorate with Finnish-made products, from Arabia dinnerware to rustic antiques. 🅐 Pöytyä. ☎ (02) 486 1807.

Piha-Puoti (Luostarinmäki Handicrafts Museum Shop) The products of these authentic workshops – candlesticks and wall hooks woven from wire, framed stained-glass panels, straw wreaths, round wooden boxes and birds made of shaved wood – are sold in the museum's shop (see page 131 for access details of the museum).

Turku Market Hall In a traditional indoor market atmosphere, 50 merchants offer speciality foods, produce and crafts.
🅐 Eerikinkatu 16. 🕐 Mon–Fri 07.00–17.30, Sat 07.00–15.00.

TAKING A BREAK

Stop at the Market Square for sausages or other quick foods. You'll also find food stalls in the market hall and at the two big open-air markets that fill Old Great Square in December and July.

Börs Café Light meals in a bright window-surrounded café just off the Market Square. 🅐 Sokos Hotel Hamburger Börs, Kauppiaskatu 6. ☎ (02) 337 381.

Café Fontana Sandwiches, cakes, light dishes, coffee and wines, served cafeteria-style in an upbeat café. 🅐 Aurakatu 1. ☎ 250 1444. 🕐 Mon–Sat 09.00–20.00, Sun 12.00–19.00.

Café Marinum Stay in the maritime spirit at the Forum Marinum, with lunch at this cheery café-restaurant. ❷ Linnankatu 72. ❶ (02) 251 0898.

Café Restaurant Aula For a break to separate the two very different worlds of medieval life and 21st-century art, stop for coffee at this tidy little museum café. ❷ Aboa Vetus & Ars Nova, Itäinen Rantakatu 4–6. ❶ (02) 279 4936. ❶ Tues–Sun 11.00–19.00.

Cafeteria Domcafé Tucked into the brick vaults below the Cathedral, this café serves excellent coffee and cakes from historic recipes. ❷ Entrance at the Cathedral steps. ❶ (02) 261 7100. ❶ Daily in summer, first three weekends in Dec.

Caffe Panini Italian panini sandwiches, pasta, pizza, salads and other light dishes, in the sophisticated setting of Casagrande House, near the river. ❷ Linnankatu 3. ❶ (02) 251 5310. ❶ Mon–Fri 11.00–22.00, Sat & Sun 12.00–22.00.

Koulu Set in a restored school (*Koulu* means 'school'), the brewery serves house beers and others, along with lunch and dinner. ❷ Eerikinkatu 18. ❶ (02) 274 5757. ❶ Sun–Thur 11.00–02.00, Fri & Sat 11.00–03.00. Food served Mon–Fri 11.00–24.00, Sat 12.00–24.00.

Pub Old Bank Everyone meets at this popular pub in an historic Jugendstil bank building, where they serve 150 different beers in an English-style bar atmosphere. The food is good, too. ❷ Aurakatu 3. ❶ (02) 274 5700. ❶ Daily from 12.00.

Puutorin Vessa Sometimes it helps if you don't speak Finnish,

especially when a pub's name translates to 'The Toilet'. This one is in a much-converted WC, hence the name – another example of the Finns' wicked sense of humour. They're serious about the food, though, and the good selection of beers. ⓐ Puutori. ① (02) 233 8123.

Surf City An internet café in the town centre, near the river. ⓐ Aninkaistenkatu 3. ① (041) 524 4330.

AFTER DARK

Along with several outstanding restaurants well worth spending an evening in, Turku has a rich cultural scene, with theatres, two orchestras, jazz clubs and rock. The Turku Music Festival and Rockfestival Ruisrock are among the oldest in Scandinavia.

Restaurants
Pavilion Vaakahuone €–€€ Go for the fish, go for the swing and Dixieland, go for the summer scene at the river. Choose from several menus all grouped around the same terrace – seafood, pizza, giant Bratwurst or a coffee shop. Live music every night. ⓐ Linnankatu 38. ① (02) 515 3321. ⓛ May–Aug daylight hours (which means most of the night in summer).

Cindyn Salonki €€ Uncomplicated dishes, many based on local seafood, are served in a boat moored on the river. ⓐ Itäinen Rantakatu. ① (02) 250 .2300. ⓦ www.cindy.fi ⓛ Mon–Fri 11.00–23.00, Sat 12.00–24.00, Sun 13.00–21.00.

Blanko €€–€€€ In the vaults of an old building near the Aurasilta Bridge, Blanko serves fusion cuisine drawn from everything from tapas to sashimi. Creative dishes include chanterelle and pumpkin lasagna or beetroot risotto. ❷ Aurakatu 1. ❶ (02) 233 3966. ❸ Daily from 11.00.

Enkeliravintola €€–€€€ The name of this restaurant translates as 'angel' and the food is indeed heavenly. Begin with a cup of warming *glogi*, while you look around at the playful decor. Then order dishes based on creative interpretations of Finnish cuisine: game terrine with lingonberries, creamy soup of forest mushrooms, *pot-au-feu* of lightly smoked pork or vegetarian mushroom pie.
❷ Kauppiaskatu 16. ❶ (02) 231 8088. ❿ www.enkeliravintola.fi

Linnankatu 3 €€–€€€ The presentation is worthy of the outstanding cuisine and surroundings; seafood dishes are superb, and the pâté is memorable. ❷ Linnankatu 3A. ❶ (02) 233 9279. ❿ www.linnankatu3.fi ❸ Mon–Fri 11.00–24.00, Sat 17.00–24.00.

Rocca €€€ Fresh local ingredients are brilliantly treated by the chef/owner – one of Finland's best-known – in dishes such as roast goose over a savoury ragout of mixed beans, and desserts such as espresso crème brulée or gingerbread sorbet. ❷ Läntinen Rantakatu 55. ❶ (02) 284 8800.

Entertainment
Galax Sleek dance/restaurant with better known Finnish performers. Minimum age is 24. ❷ Aurakatu 6. ❶ (02) 284 3300.

Sibelius Museum Chamber Concerts Chamber music concerts are held each Wednesday evening in the atrium (except in summer). ❷ Piispankatu 17. ❶ (02) 215 4494. ❿ www.sibeliusmuseum.abo.fi

ACCOMMODATION

Best Western Hotel Seaport € Located in a charming converted customs warehouse right in the dock area, this makes a good choice if you are cruising in or out of Turku on a Baltic ferry. The rooms are attractive and comfortable; the whole place was updated and renovated in 2004. ⓐ Matkustajasatama. ⓣ (02) 283 3000. ⓕ (02) 283 3100. ⓦ www.bestwestern.com

Ruissalo Spa Hotel €€ Pamper youself at this elegant spa on Ruissalo Island. A large, modern resort, its rooms are smart and there are several restaurants. The sport and spa facilities are superb. It sits amidst walking, jogging and cycling trails and beaches and is close to an 18-hole golf course. ⓐ Ruissalon puistotie 640. ⓣ (02) 445 5100. ⓕ (02) 445 5101. ⓦ www.ruissalospa.fi

Naantali Spa Resort €€–€€€ Saunas and aromatic aquatherapy are only the beginning of the facilities offered at this state-of-the-art resort spa near Turku. From the huge indoor pool, dive under the glass wall and stare at the winter sky from a steaming outdoor pool. ⓐ Naantali. ⓣ (02) 445 5100. ⓦ www.naantalispa.fi

Sokos Hotel Hamburger Börs €€–€€€ You could hardly find a hotel closer to the centre of activity in this handsome town than the 346 rooms overlooking Market Square. These are nicely appointed in modern Scandinavian style. There are three saunas, a pool and other leisure facilities for guests, as well as seven restaurants. ⓐ Kauppiaskatu 6. ⓣ (02) 337 381. ⓕ (02) 23 1010. ⓦ www.sokoshotels.fi

---

ⓞ *Helsinki Railway Station has Eliel Saarinen's most famous interior*

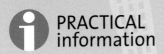

PRACTICAL
information

Directory

GETTING THERE

Helsinki can be reached by direct daily flights from major European hubs. Its location on the Baltic makes boat a popular way to get there from Stockholm and from ports in Estonia and Germany. Most of these ferries also carry cars, so Finland can be incorporated into a driving holiday.

By air

From the UK and Europe Finnair offers the most options, with several daily flights from Heathrow to Vantaa and some direct flights from Manchester. Ryanair flies from Stansted to Tampere, often at unbelievably low fares. SAS and British Airways also have daily flights direct to Vantaa from Heathrow. Finnair operates daily direct flights from JFK in New York and in the summer, from Toronto. SAS flies from several US gateways, but always connecting through Stockholm or Copenhagen.

Finnair 🕿 🕅 www.finnair.com
Ryanair 🕅 www. ryanair.com
SAS 🕅 www.scandinavian.net
British Airways 🕅 www.britishairways.com

By rail

Train travel is possible as far as Stockholm, from which point you must take a ferry. The trip from London's Waterloo International to Stockholm takes just over 18 hours, by Eurostar to Brussels, with changes in Cologne, Hamburg and Copenhagen, and the trains boarding ferries for the water crossings. The monthly *Thomas Cook European Rail Timetable* has up-to-date schedules for European

international and national train services. Travellers from outside
Europe who plan to use trains should investigate the various multi-
day and multi-country train passes offered by Rail Europe. Eurail
Selectpass includes rail travel in all four Scandinavian countries
(or any combination of them) plus Germany, with even greater
savings for two or more people travelling together.

Eurostar ❶ 08705 186186 (UK). Ⓦ www.eurostar.com

Thomas Cook European Rail Timetable ❶ (UK) (01733) 416477;
(USA) 1 800 322 3834. Ⓦ www.thomascookpublishing.com

Rail Europe Ⓦ www.raileurope.com

⬇ *Vantaa is Helsinki's modern gateway*

By ferry

Sweden, Germany, Estonia and St Petersburg are all connected to Finland by ferry links. The main shipping lines operating these are Viking, Silja and Superfast Ferries, which operates the route from Rostock, Germany, to Hanko, 90 minutes from Helsinki. Service from Rostock and Stockholm is offered daily, year-round. DFDS in Newcastle) operates ferries to other Scandinavian ports, from which connections to Finland are possible, but time-consuming.

Viking Ⓦ www.vikingline.fi

Silja Ⓦ www.silja.fi

Superfast Ferries Ⓦ www.superfast.com

DFDS ❶ (0191) 293 6209 in the UK. Ⓦ www.dfdsseaways.co.uk

By bus

Next to a lucky hit for rock-bottom air fare, the cheapest way to Helsinki from the UK is by bus, again via Stockholm, about 35 hours from London's Victoria Coach Station via Eurolines. From Stockholm you must take a ferry to Finland.

Eurolines ❶ 08705 143219. Ⓦ www.gobycoach.com or www.eurolines.com

Driving

Car trips to Finland from the UK must include at least one crossing by car ferry, which adds significantly to the cost. But this remains a budget-friendly option if several people are travelling together. The shortest route, the Via Baltica, is to Tallinn, Estonia, making the final short crossing on one of the several daily car ferries to Helsinki.

Finland, like the rest of the continent, drives on the right-hand side of the road. Keep a sharp eye out for elks and/or reindeer on the road outside urban areas. Serious – many of them fatal – accidents occur each year when vehicles hit large animals. When animals weighing several hundred kilos crash through a windscreen, it's not a pretty sight.

ENTRY FORMALITIES
Passports & visas
Citizens of the Uk, Republic of Ireland, USA, Canada and Australia need only a valid passport to enter Finland and do not require visas. Citizens of EU countries other than the UK need only a valid national identity card, or a passport. Citizens of South Africa must have passport and visas to enter. Visa forms can be obtained from your nearest Finnish embassy or consulate.

Customs regulations
EU citizens can bring goods for personal use when arriving from another EU country, but must observe the limits on tobacco (800 cigarettes) and spirits (10 litres of alcohol over 22 per cent proof, 20 litres of wine). Limits for non-EU nationals are 200 cigarettes and 1 litre of spirits, 2 litres of wine.

MONEY
The currency in Finland is the euro (€), which is divided into 100 cents. Notes are in € 5, 20, 50, 100 and 500 denominations and coins are € 1, 2, and 5, and 10, 20 and 50 cents. The best means of obtaining local currency is by using a debit card. Although many banks charge a fee for this, these are usually less than cash advances on credit cards, and are at a more favourable exchange rate than cash transactions or traveller's cheques. ATMs (cashpoints) can be found nearly everywhere, easily recognized by yellow hoods. Finns call an ATM an *otto*.

Credit cards are very widely used in Helsinki, even by taxis, and you can often pay by credit card in pubs and get cash back if you're short. Traveller's cheques can be cashed at banks, post offices and in most hotels, and are widely accepted in major shops and stores in Helsinki.

Currency exchange services are in airports and near the central railway station. There is a Travelex exchange booth at the Vantaa Airport International Terminal (🕿 (09) 6151 3852). Helsinki's main bank is Nordea (most central branch: ➋ Aleksanterinkatu 52, 🕿 (02) 003 000). Banking hours are usually Mon–Fri 09.30–16.15.

HEALTH, SAFETY & CRIME

Finnish medical care is excellent, with English-speaking doctors and modern clinics and hospitals. Free emergency service is available to all visitors. Those from EU (and a few other European countries) are

treated free if they have brought an EHIC card. Obtain this from a local post office before leaving home. Those without an EHIC must pay for services. EU residents are recommended, nevertheless, to take out adequate travel insurance before departing, and for non-EU travellers it is an absolute necessity.

If you are there in the winter and take part in winter sports, remember that the thickness of ice on lakes and bays is hard to judge. Skate or walk on ice only with a trained guide or where a number of others are also on the ice. Never venture onto ice alone, even if you think you are sure of its strength.

Finland is one of the safest countries to travel in, but remember that wherever tourists gather, there will be occasional pickpockets (perhaps visitors themselves). Lock valuables in the hotel safe or

⬤ *Gigantic art nouveau guardians of Helsinki Railway Station*

leave them at home. You are not likely to need your diamond tiara in Helsinki.

TOILETS

Public facilities are common in Helsinki, but they may not be open all hours. Those inside buildings such as the public markets close with the market. Those in parks may be open limited hours and closed Sunday and in the winter. Those in hotels and cafés are a good alternative when others are closed.

CHILDREN

Finns are fond of children and frequently take their own with them, so most hotels and restaurants are prepared. Those with music and entertainment, as well as other nightspots, do not welcome children, any more than their equivalents would in any city. However, Helsinki has plenty of family-friendly attractions.

- **Linnanmäki Amusement Park** and its Sea Life Centre are close to the centre of Helsinki and especially designed for children, with rides, a monorail, an open-air theatre, eating places that welcome children, and a free playground. Sea Life Centre explores marine life with aquatic adventures. And to make you feel good about every euro you spend on rides, all the income goes to the national child welfare organisations that run the park. ❸ Tivolikuja 1. ❶ (09) 773 991. ❹ Apr–Sept, hours vary with season. Admission charge according to children's age and height, separately at each ride. ❷ Tram/bus 3T or 23.

- **Korkeasaari Zoo** is worthwhile for the entire family, with rare cats (including snow leopards), red pandas, a specialist collection of animals indigenous to the Arctic and, by contrast, many Amazonian species in the Amazonia micro-climate house. The trip there by ferry is fun for children, too. ⓐ Korkeasaari. ⓣ (09) 169 5969, ⓦ www.zoo.hel.fi. ⓛ Daily. 10.00–20.00 May–Sept; 10.00–16.00 Oct–Feb, 10.00–18.00 Mar–Apr. Admission charge (free for under-7s). ⓝ Ferry daily May–Sept from Market Square, or Hakaniemi Market, Bus 11 (summer and weekends winter) or, on winter weekdays, bus 16 or metro to Kulosaari, then a 1.5 km (1 mile) walk.

- **Serena Waterpark** is a bit out of town, but reachable by bus. This is a good diversion if the weather turns hot in the summer, or when you need a breath of the tropics on a wintry day. Children won't believe that a water park stays open in the winter. It's a low-key splash park, but good for young children. ⓐ Tornimäentie 10, Espoo. ⓣ (09) 8870 5557. ⓛ Daily 11.00–20.00. Admission charge (free for under-4s). ⓝ Bus 339 from Helsinki bus station.

- **Lego Show Helsinki** You'll like playing in this Lego wonderland just as much as the kids do. Plenty of access to all the hands-on activities is assured by timed ticketing. Choose your 3-hour time slot, at 11.00–14.00, 14.00–17.00 or 17.00–20.00. ⓐ Coca Cola Centre, Sörnäisten rantatie 6, at Hakaniemi Market Square. ⓣ (09) 2706 6640. ⓛ Daily May–Aug 10.00–20.00. Admission charge. ⓝ Bus/tram 68, 23N or 97N.

Performances for children are staged on Suomenlinna island during the summer, with a variety of shows and theatre companies participating. The Helsinki City Tourist & Convention Bureau will have schedules. Older children will enjoy exploring the fortress and, as with the zoo, the boat ride there is an adventure itself. They will also enjoy the hands-on activities at Seurasaari Open-air Museum, as well as the unusual old buildings.

COMMUNICATIONS

Phones

Mobile phones are almost universal, and European, New Zealand and Australian mobiles can link to several GSM networks after changing the band. US and Canadian mobile phones do not work in Finland unless they are specially equipped before leaving North America. Because of the high use of mobile phones in Finland (the highest per capita in the world), public telephones are getting harder and harder to find. The best places to find them are the railway and bus station, shopping centres and large department stores. Phone cards are still available from the main information desks in the railway and bus stations and in large department stores and at some hotel reception desks.

The country code for Finland is 358. The city code for Helsinki is 09, for Turku 02, for Porvoo 019. To call from outside Finland, dial the international access code of the country you're calling from (usually 00), then 358 and then the Finnish city code (omitting the first 0), e.g. 00 358 9 for Helsinki, and then the number. From inside Finland, dial the city code and number. To make an international call from Finland, dial 00, then the country code (UK 44, Republic of Ireland 353, USA and Canada 1, Australia 61, New Zealand 64, South Africa 27) and the area code (omitting the initial zero in UK area codes) and then the number.

Post

Finnish post is not only prompt, it is safe; the Finns are honest to their toes, so what you mail will arrive safely and quickly. Each city or town's main post office has poste restante service, so letters and parcels can be sent to the post office with the recipient's name and post office address marked 'Poste Restante'. Mail will be held for a month before being returned. Helsinki's main post office is Posti Central Office ✆ Elielinaukio 2. ☎ 9800 7100 (free within Finland). 🕐 Mon–Fri 07.00–21.00, Sat & Sun 10.00–18.00. It costs €0.65 to send a postcard, which should arrive within 3–4 days in the EU and a week in North America.

Internet

Public internet access is widely available in larger towns, with public libraries offering access, in addition to internet cafés. Many hotels have internet available for guests. Stockmann department store has computers in its cybercafé Brutal, but there are often long queues waiting to use them. Other internet cafés include:

Waynes Coffee ✆ Kaisaniemenkatu 3. ☎ (09) 6843 2310.
🕐 Mon–Fri 08.00–21.00, Sat 10.00–21.00, Sun 12.00–21.00.

Mbar Internet café with DJs and performances at night.
✆ Lasipalatsi/Mannerheimintie 22–24. ☎ (09) 6124 5420.
🕐 Mon & Tues 09.00–24.00, Wed & Thur 09.00–02.00, Fri & Sat 09.00–03.00, Sun 12.00–24.00.

ELECTRICITY

Current in Finland is 220V AC, at 50 Hz. Australian, New Zealand, US, Canadian and some South African and UK appliances will need adapters to fit Finnish wall outlets. If you are travelling in other Scandinavian countries, note that outlets are not all the same. Appliances using only 110V will need transformers, as well as plug adapters.

MEDIA

Helsinki's newspaper *Helsingin Sanomat* publishes an an English-language version, good for local news and events. International newspapers are available at news-stands and in hotels. For events, see the free weekly magazine in English, *Helsinki This Week*.

TRAVELLERS WITH DISABILITIES

Lifts provide access to all floors (including the subterranean tunnels that connect much of the central area) in the major department stores and shopping centres, as well as the railway station and Kinopalatsi Cinema Centre. When using the tunnels, you can access street level through these buildings or by a number of lifts throughout the system. For a listing of these locations, as well as excellent maps, see ⓦ http://esteeton.teho.net This handy site also lists public toilets with full access, car parks and tourist sights with access information, in English. The zoo, Suomenlinna fortress, the Atheneum and a number of other tourist sights have disabled access to most of their facilities, as do the opera house and Finlandia Hall. The outdoor areas of Seurasaari Open-air Museum are accessible, but the historic buildings are not.

There is normally a space in Finnish trains for wheelchairs, as well as a special table, allowing for wheelchair manoeuvres. These spaces need reservations, but there is normally no extra charge.

For specially equipped taxis, call one of the following:

Helsingin Invakuljetus Oy ⓐ Helsingin Palveluauto. ⓣ (09) 350 5200
Invataxi Iiro's Taxi Service Ltd ⓣ (09) 4114 2070 or (040) 500 6070.

FURTHER INFORMATION
Tourist offices
Helsinki City Tourist & Convention Bureau ⓐ Pohjoisesplanadi 19,

Helsinki. ☎ (09) 169.3757. 🖷 (09) 169 3839. 🌐 www.hel.fi/tourism
🕐 Mon–Fri 09.00–20.00, Sat & Sun 09.00–18.00 May–Sept;
Mon–Fri 09.00–18.00, Sat & Sun 10.00–16.00 Oct–Apr.

Finnish Tourist Board ✉ PO Box 33213, London W6 8JX. ☎ (020) 7365
2512. 🖷 (020) 8600 5681. 🌐 www.visitfinland.com/uk

Embassy of Finland ✉ 38 Chesham Place, London SW1X 8HW.
☎ (020) 7838 6200. 🖷 (020) 7235 3680. 🌐 www.finemb.org.uk

Finnish Tourist Board ✉ 655 Third Avenue, New York, NY 10017.
☎ (212) 885 9735. 🌐 www.gofinland.org

🔽 *Ferries drop their passengers right into the very heart of Helsinki*

Useful phrases

These Finnish words and phrases may come in handy. See also the phrases for specific situations in other parts of the book.

English	Finnish	Approx. pronunciation
BASICS		
Yes	Joo	*Yoo*
No	Ei	*Aye*
Thank you	Kiitos	*Keetoss*
Hello	Hei	*Hey*
Goodbye	Näkemiin	*Nakehmeen*
Excuse me	Anteeksi	*Erntehksi*
Sorry	Sori	*Sorry*
That's okay	Ole hyvä	*Oleh hewva*
Do you speak English?	Puhutko englantia?	*Puhutko ehnglerntier?*
Good morning	Hyvää huomenta	*Hewva-a huomehnter*
Good afternoon	Hyvää päivää	*Hewva-a pa-i-va-a*
Good evening	Hyvää iltaa	*Hewva-a iltah*
Goodnight	Hyvää yötä	*Hewva-a ew-erta*
My name is ...	Minun nimeni on ...	*Minun nimehni on ...*
DAYS & TIMES		
Monday	Maanantai	*Deftera*
Tuesday	Tiistai	*Triti*
Wednesday	Keskiviikko	*Tetarti*
Thursday	Torstai	*Pembti*
Friday	Perjantai	*Paraskevi*
Saturday	Lauantai	*Savvato*
Sunday	Sunnuntai	*Kiriaki*
Morning	Aamu	*Proi*
Afternoon	Iltapäivällä	*Apoyevma*
Night	Yö	*Nihta*
Yesterday	Eilen	*Htes*

English	Finnish	Approx. pronunciation
Today	Tänään	Tana-an
Tomorrow	Huomenna	Huo-mehn-ner
What time is it?	Paljonko kello on?	Perlyonko kehl-lo on?
It is ...	Kello on ...	Kehl-lo on ...
Midday	Keskipäivä	Kehski-pa-i-va
Midnight	Keskiyö	Kehski-ewer

NUMBERS

One	Yksi	Ewksi
Two	Kaksi	Kerksi
Three	Kolme	Kolmeh
Four	Neljä	Nehlyah
Five	Viisi	Veesi
Six	Kuusi	Koosi
Seven	Seitsemän	Sehtsehman
Eight	Kahdeksan	Kerdehksern
Nine	Yhdeksän	Ewkh-dehksan
Ten	Kymmenen	Kewmehnehn
Twenty	Kaksikymmentä	Kerksi-kew-mehnta
Fifty	Viisikymmentä	Veesi-kew-mehnta
One hundred	Sata	Ser-ter
One thousand	Tuhat	Tu-hert

MONEY

I would like to change these traveller's cheques/this currency	Haluaisin vaihtaa rahaa/matkashekkejä	Her-lu-aisin vaikh-tah rer-hah/mertker-shehk-kehja
What's the exchange rate?	Mikä on kurssi?	Mi-kah on kurs-si?
Credit card	Luottokortti	Luot-tokort-ti

SIGNS & NOTICES

Airport	Lentokenttä
Smoking/non-smoking	Tupakointi /Tupakointi kielletty
Toilets	WC
Open/Closed	Auki/Suljeti

Emergencies

EMERGENCY NUMBERS
Police, ambulance or fire 112

Medical emergencies
Should you become ill in Finland, you have several sources of information on English-speaking doctors – although you will find that most speak rather good English. The consular office of your embassy can provide a list. You can also go prepared with the appropriate pages from the directory published by the International Association of Medical Assistance for Travellers (IAMAT), a non-profit organisation that provides information on health-related travel issues all over the world, as well as lists of English speaking doctors ⓦ www.iamat.org

24-hour medical and dental treatment can be obtained at:
Hospital Mehiläinen ⓐ Pohjoinen Hesperiankatu 17. ⓣ (010) 414 4210.

Police
Main police station For non-urgent police assistance.
ⓐ Punanotkonkatu 2.
The most central precinct is at ⓐ Pieni Roobertinkatu 1–3.
ⓣ (09) 1891.

Lost property
Police Lost Property Office ⓐ Paijanteentie 12A. ⓣ (09) 189 3180.
ⓛ Mon–Fri 08.00–16.15. ⓞ Tram 7B.
Transport Lost Property For items lost on trains, buses, trams and at the airport. You can make enquiries by telephone. ⓐ Kauppiaankatu 8–10. ⓣ 0600 410 06. ⓛ Mon–Fri 09.00–18.00.

EMERGENCY PHRASES

Help!   **Help me, please!**
Apua!   Voitko auttaa!
Erpuer!   *Voytko owttah!*

Call an ambulance/Call a doctor/Call the police!
Soittakaaa ambulanssi/Kutsukaa lääkäri/ Soittakaaa poliisi!
Soi-terkah ermbulernsi/Kutsukah lahkari/ Soi-terkah polleesi!

CONSULATES & EMBASSIES

Consulates and consular sections of embassies handle emergencies of travelling citizens. Your consulate or embassy should be the first place you turn to if a passport is lost, after reporting it to the police.

British Embassy 🅰️ Itäinen Puistotie 17. ☎️ (09) 228 65100, 228 65210 or 2286 5216. For emergencies outside normal hours (0500) 817 242, 🌐 www.britishembassy.fi 🕐 Mon–Fri. 08.30–15.00 late June–late Aug; 09.00–17.00 rest of year.

Canadian Embassy 🅰️ Pohjoisesplanadi 25B. ☎️ (09) 228 530.
☎️ (09) 601 060. ✉️ hsnki@international.gc.ca 🌐 www.canada.fi

Irish Embassy 🅰️ Erottajankatu 7A. ☎️ (09) 646 006.

New Zealand Consulate 🅰️ Kohdematkat Oy, Hietalahdenranta 13. ☎️ (09) 615 615.

South African Embassy 🅰️ Rahapajankatu 1 A 5 (3rd Floor).
☎️ (09) 6860 3100. 🕐 Consular hours: Mon–Fri 09.00–14.00.

United States Embassy, Consular Office 🅰️ Itäinen Puistotie 14B.
☎️ (09) 6162 5701. ✉️ helsinkiACS@state.gov 🌐 www.usembassy.fi
🕐 Mon–Thur 09.00–12.00. Phone hours Mon–Fri 08:30–17.00.

The author would like to thank University of Helsinki Almanac Office for supplying data on public holidays.

The publishers would like to thank the following individuals for their contribution in the production of this book:
A1 Pix: pages 7, 23, 33, 61, 108 and 153.
Finnish Tourist Board: pages 5, 18, 28, 35, 46, 53, 93, 100 and 143.
Stillman Rogers Photography: pages 1, 9, 12, 15. 17, 21, 39, 42, 49, 67, 70, 78, 81, 88, 90, 116, 123, 124, 127, 135, 141 and 146.
Copy-editor: Stephen York
Proofreader: Colin Follett

Send your thoughts to
books@thomascook.com

- **Found a great bar, club, shop or must-see sight that we don't feature?**

- **Like to tip us off about any information that needs a little updating?**

- **Want to tell us what you love about this handy little guidebook and more importantly how we can make it even handier?**

Then here's your chance to tell all! Send us ideas, discoveries and recommendations today and then look out for your valuable input in the next edition of this title. As an extra 'thank you' from Thomas Cook Publishing, you'll be automatically entered into our exciting monthly prize draw.

Email the above address (stating the book's title) or write to:
CitySpots Project Editor, Thomas Cook Publishing, PO Box 227, Unit 15/16, Coningsby Road, Peterborough PE3 8SB, UK.